Headstrong

HEADSTRONG

Women Porters, Blackness, and Modernity in Accra

Laurian R. Bowles

PENN

UNIVERSITY OF PENNSYLVANIA PRESS

PHILADELPHIA

Published by
University of Pennsylvania Press
Philadelphia, Pennsylvania 19104–4112 USA
www.pennpress.org

EU Authorized Representative: Easy Access System
Europe - Mustamäe tee 50, 10621 Tallinn, Estonia,
gpsr.requests@easproject.com

Printed in the United States of America on acid-free paper

10 9 8 7 6 5 4 3 2 1

A Cataloging-in-Publication record for this book is
available from the Library of Congress.

Paperback ISBN 978-1-5128-2465-0
Hardcover ISBN 978-1-5128-2464-3
Ebook ISBN 978-1-5128-2466-7

CONTENTS

Introduction

I learned my way through the sprawling alleys, lanes, and corridors of Accra's city center markets around the same time Zaynab Keidu traveled from Ghana's hinterland to work as a porter in the capital. It was 2007 when Zaynab arrived at Tema Station, one of the three transit stations that encircle Makola, the city's largest consumer market. Arriving at the depot in the afternoon, Zaynab gathered a medium-sized checkered bag from under her seat and began her walk toward the swelling informal settlements at Agbogbloshie. An hour after her arrival, and despite her best effort to follow the directions provided by her hometown neighbor, who now lived in Accra, Zaynab was lost. The dizzying cacophony of sounds and teeming crowd of people moving about were disorienting. The orange haze of dusk pushed time against her. Zaynab was exhausted from the twelve-hour journey, which had included two bus changes. The one-hour walk turned into three hours of being lost. Night had fallen, and the night sky barely glowed from the city lights. The streets were dim except for the headlights of passing cars.

As Zaynab rounded the roasted-corn seller for the second time, she also noticed women passersby wearing hijabs and speaking Hausa and Dagbanli. These cues prompted Zaynab to inquire about where she might be able to sleep for the night. Weary and anxious, Zaynab struck up a conversation with a group of young women as they walked by. They carried metal basins or large pieces of plywood, which indicated their work status as porters. Zaynab was relieved when a group of women settling behind a stack of wooden pallets invited her to join them for a night's rest. She introduced herself to her fellow migrants from the north, and a wave of relief washed over her when someone offered her some food. It was Zaynab's first trip to Accra, and she was grateful not to have to figure out dinner after having been lost the last few hours. She didn't have a cell phone, but one of the women, Amena, directed her to the nearby call center to notify her family of her safe arrival. As she escorted her, Amena warned Zaynab not to trust the generosity of strangers.

Although in her late teens, Zaynab had never slept in the company of anyone who was not a close relative. After calling her mother, who thanked Allah for her safe arrival, and realizing that she was now preparing to sleep outdoors, under the stars, with a group of strangers, Zaynab was terrified. With no options to heed Amena's warning and too weary from the five-hundred-mile trip, Zaynab took her chances with the seven women who had agreed to let her squat with them.

Zaynab spoke three languages and heard each one less frequently on her southward journey to Accra, so her ears perked when she heard a familiar tone and tenor as she approached the woodpile. A conversation was underway; she heard someone chiding another for bringing Zaynab to their sleep space. Zaynab stepped back into the area, pretending not to hear the exchange. Instead, she copied what everyone was doing and spread a cloth on the ground. She wedged her bundle of clothes underneath her sore back and tucked her flip-flops between her thighs and inside the folds of her ankle-length skirt. Determined to find her neighbor the next day, Zaynab fell asleep with a mix of fright and gratitude.

The next morning, when Zaynab awakened, all the women were gone and so was her footwear. Her remaining bundle of clothes, still tucked underneath her, was a small consolation. Now barefoot, Zaynab gathered up her things and stepped from behind the stack of plywood to resume her search. She wound through the maze of the onion market, through the sprawling waste piles of Agbogbloshie, until she found her neighbor, who had worriedly stayed home from work to wait for her arrival. The woman immediately sent someone to buy Zaynab another pair of flip-flops while giving her something to eat. Exhausted again, Zaynab slept several hours in the lean-to her neighbor rented with four other porters. The following day, just before dawn, Zaynab fetched a bucket of water for her morning ablutions, picked up a slat of plywood, and followed her neighbor to join the thousands of women who transport goods through the pedestrian labyrinth of Makola Market, beginning her new job as a head porter.

Over the last fifteen years, I have often listened to Zaynab share her Accra arrival story. In a 2013 retelling, Zaynab chuckled at the aptness of the Call Mama Communication Centre, where she did indeed call to speak with her mother. When Zaynab shared her story in 2018, we were at lunch in a restaurant near Atta Mills High Street, just around the corner from where Zaynab slept on that first night, years ago. Zaynab no longer does porter work and now runs a pop-up daycare to babysit for women who want relief from carrying their children on their backs while they head-load. Zaynab's now-calm composure belied the fright that punctuated her voice a decade earlier. The first time she talked to me about coming to Accra, she was only a few months removed from her initiation to the city, and her story then focused on the persistence of mosquitoes and her cold fear of being so far from home.

"Here in Accra, hospitality and accommodation are not stable," said Zaynab, between bites of food. "Being from the north got me a space to sleep, but it didn't stop them from taking my things."

When Zaynab first told me her arrival story in 2007, her body shook as she recalled her hazing welcome to Accra, an ambivalent experience. Encouraged to come to the city after witnessing the influx of remittances sent by her neighbor, Zaynab was disgusted by the swarm of new smells that assailed her as she walked through the market and its surrounding neighborhoods. She was impressed by the ease with which her neighbor replaced her footwear but unsettled by the spectral qualities of the previous night's sleep arrangements. Grateful not to have slept alone on her first night in the city, Zaynab was hurt by the women's mistrust and theft on her first night in the city.

With her frequent retelling of her arrival story, Zaynab skillfully explores a spectrum of emotion, from a sense of belonging to fear of harm, offering reflections on the interiority of feeling out of place. Zaynab unraveled the somatic, affective, and spatial registers of what it means, and feels like, to be a porter in Accra and vividly captured how identity and locale quickly pivot to a sense of exclusion and inclusion. Then and now, and like many other porters, Zaynab grapples with an irreconcilable difference between her aspirations and the realities of her livelihood.

Porters regularly make decisions informed by circumstances beyond their control and then, through stories, reflect on the events surrounding their choices, which is why I chose Zaynab's arrival narrative as the entrée to the foundational theories and methods of this book. Drawing on over a decade of fieldwork grounded in African feminisms and Black feminism, *Headstrong* examines the physical, emotional, and spatial aspects of porterage—the labor of carrying loads—and the lived experiences of women porters in Accra, Ghana. A city with a long history as a diasporic home and a bourgeoning travel destination, Accra grapples with material and dialectic struggles around growth and change. Tourism websites, unironically, tout Ghana as a gem of West Africa (Germansky 2017): English is the lingua franca, hospitality is considered a Ghanaian cultural dictate, and a seaside cabana is just a short drive from the recently renovated Kotoka Airport. The recent infrastructural boom includes new roadways, high-rise office complexes, shopping malls, and luxury hotels. Residential sprawl in freshly erected neighborhoods like Airport City has stretched the city limits. Sophisticated hot spots, frequented by expats and domestic multinationals, dot the well-heeled areas of Cantonments, Dzorwulu, East Legon, and Airport Residential.

Knowledge about the how poor women make a living in this gentrified city is instructive for understanding what constitutes belonging and social entitlement in an African city. With a focus on everyday habits, attitudes, and practices, *Headstrong* explains how the social differences that manufacture porters as the foil to progress miss how *kayayei*[1] are the vanguard for thinking through the residual legacies of slavery and colonialism in Ghana. Conceptualizations of blackness, rooted in the colonial era and the transatlantic slave trade, persist in contemporary forms of capitalist accumulation and expropriation and are rendered through the bodies of women laborers in Ghanaian markets. Anthropologists have long argued about how the West has remade modernity in its image as a rationale for capitalist interests in resource extraction and the accumulation of raw materials (Mafeje 1998). In many instances, modernity remains conceptualized in Africa as something unfolding or forthcoming, with the continent viewed as a "natural laboratory against which European theories of modernity are tested" (Jili 2022; see also Enwezor 2010). As an "ideology that blends capitalist interests with colonialism and coloniality," modernity is also a placeholder for the racial scripts that inform everyday life (Tamale 2020, xv). But rather than giving an ethnographic account of the city and its relationships to modernity, the book situates women porters at Makola Market, the largest open-air market in Accra, as chronotopes of modernity who help assemble the racial and spatial logistics of gendered trade.[2] All around various markets, the movement of goods, carried on the heads of women, is a rhythmic representation of vibrant commerce. As witness to how porters confront, demur to, and uncover the frail and false promises of city life and the racial and gendered scripts that underscore their social relationships, this book examines how colonial ideologies are repurposed in social cues about gender, class, locale, and sexual politics. Through conversations, interviews, and observations of work relationships, intimate relationships, sleeping arrangements, and the labor of head-loading, *Headstrong* reveals how social calculi of difference animates entitlements to the city as a place of home and a site of work. As an ethnography of sense and sensibilities and their relationships to the places that structure the labor of women when they are in Accra, *Headstrong* also measures how precarity is reproduced and enforced while simultaneously operating as naturalized harm in Accra.

Accra is a popular hub for West African migrants who seek work at one of the two dozen markets that operate in the capital. Makola Market is the city's most comprehensive shopping district for consumer goods. Women dominate the market, ranging from multigenerational groups of women traders to street hawkers and head porters. Thousands of women engage in market work daily, and there is no shortage of ethnography about the women who hold sway in Ghanaian street markets (see Asiedu and Agyei-Mensah 2008; Clark 1994; House-Midamba and Ekechi 1995; Robertson 1983). For instance, the iconic documentary *Asante Market Women* (1982) contrasts market women's domestic and public lives, where traders are household subordinates in polygamous marriages but tough negotiators and skillful politicians at the market. The film's representation situates the market trader as having "a truncated life based on her gender," while simultaneously insisting on the market as *the* central space for women to reclaim social entitlements eroded by patriarchy (Ebron 2007, 182). In some ways, this private-public dichotomy around women's personas, showcased in the film, is concurrent with the scholarship on gender in Ghana. African markets are protofeminist spaces: sites where equity is engendered, empowering of women, and essential for feeding and clothing the nation. And then there are ways that, within that sphere of emancipatory possibility, markets are also classed, racialized, ethnically oriented, and regionally specific (Oyĕwùmí 1997). *Headstrong* aims to ethnographically situate both of these truths.

If Accra is the harbinger of a lively and welcoming African city, it is also a forerunner of the neoliberal austerities of shrinking public safety nets and depressed wages (Honwana 2012). Strangers quickly become co-complainants in lamentations about traffic congestion, the murderous floods of the rainy season, exorbitant food prices, housing insecurity, houselessness, and house unaffordability (Ofosu-Kusi and Danso-Wiredu 2014; Owusu-Sekyere and Amoah 2020). Ghana's remarkable economic growth has not led to widespread or equitable increases in employment. Tourism, the growing entrenchment of foreign investments, and the liberalized import market all engender a surplus labor economy that struggles against prolonged household insecurity and intergenerational poverty. While the scholarship on labor and migration often conceives of the informal economy as a hindrance to the growth of the employment sector; this perspective overlooks the ravages of neoliberalism and the creative efforts of the people who live in its wake.

Accra has been a repository for domestic and regional migrants for hundreds of years (Grier 1992). Thousands of people travel to Accra each year to seek work in the proliferating service economies. Since the colonial Gold Coast, the city has been a cornerstone of capital accumulation and dispossession. During British colonization, head-loading became waged labor when men and women were hired to transport raw materials to the coast for expropriation. Before efficiently extracting colonial railways were completed, head-loading was the most successful way to move goods from the interior to the beach (Tsey 2013). In the 1920s, the British relied on male and female porters to streamline cocoa expropriation (Grier 1992). Colonialists also instituted coercive communal labor to strengthen gold-extraction sectors and boost plantation agriculture during the same period (Akurang-Parry 2000).

Market liberalizations of the last thirty years, driven by structural adjustment programs that diminish domestic market protections, led to an influx of cheap foreign goods that expanded consumer demand and thus a steady increase of porters at work in Accra. In 2007, estimates suggested 25,000 girls and women worked as porters at Accra markets (Bayor 2007; Boakye-Boaten 2008). At the 2022 National Kayayei Dialogue hosted by the Henry Djaba Foundation (with support from the United Nations Population Fund), the number cited was 160,000 girl and women porters in Ghana, half of them at work in Accra. The part of Ghana's transportation sector reliant on the movement of products in metal basins or on pieces of plywood balanced on heads also includes commercial buses, *trotros* (minibuses), motorcycles, and wheelbarrows (Agarwal et al. 1997), all suffused with gendered divisions of labor.

Driving taxis, buses, and *trotros* is constructed as a masculine labor task,[3] while head-loading, a specifically feminized habit, is associated with household labor wherein girls and women are tasked with fetching water or collecting firewood (Grieco, Apt, and Turner 1996). This household-based feminization extends to porter work, which, although the most effective and efficient way to move goods in a tightly ordered market, has a gendered differentiation with inequitable consequences. *Kaya* work is considered a "low-skilled job" held by "low-skilled" workers,[4] but when boys and men porter, they use assistive transportation technologies such as wheelbarrows and hand trucks. On the other hand, the girls and women who porter *become* technology by mechanizing their bodies to carry loads. Even the naming convention (*kayayei*) flattens girls and women within the larger feminization of the markets and endorses head porterage as essential yet devalued (Grier 1992).

Accra has innumerable identities and valuations among its four million inhabitants, and the "impulse to valorize cities as commodities" makes aluminum basins a helpful metaphor for understanding Ghana's capital (Arthur 2018, 4). One of the most familiar images of African women is a photo or painting of a woman balancing items on her head, with a colorful cloth folded in a doughnut shape to cushion against the burdensome load she carries. The heaviness of the metal pans, silver-gray in color or speckled white and robin's-egg blue, depends on the amount of aluminum used to manufacture them (Agbola 2013). The broad utility, lifespan, and affordability of aluminum basins mean they are always in use. Prices range from 60 to 200 cedis (US$10–30), and larger basins have a thirty-inch diameter and are approximately twelve inches deep. Irrespective of whether it is in relation to motorized or nonmotorized transportation, the girls and women who carry aluminum pans are *the* critical labor force to the market's and city's supply chains. On any given day, their loading pans, in addition to being the vessel to transport goods, may also transport water, wash clothes, bathe children, serve as a cooking pan, or keep perishables cool. As Vida Asomaning et al. point out, "In Accra, 'the load women carry' is not simply an expression, a figure of speech for the tedium and toil that is women's lot, but a virtual description of their task as porters" (1996, 59), so it is with ease that so many girls and women leave home to enter head-loading work as transporters (Opare 2003). As domestic migrants from rural areas, porters usually spend the growing seasons at work off the farm. As families await harvest of groundnuts, okra, sorghum, and yams on their family farms, women leave with the blessing (or expectations) of their families, to head-load and send remittances. Others are unmarried girls and women who hope to earn enough money to pay school fees, purchase household goods to be considered marriageable, or garner enough seed money for their entrepreneurial endeavors. The spatial tightness of markets demands constant improvisations, which creates an ongoing reliance on porters to keep transportation overhead down. Large-scale, bulk, or wholesale items, such as produce or construction materials, need to move from delivery trucks to warehouses. Smaller items rely on porters and their metal basins to distribute high volumes to stores, stalls, and hawkers. Porters also transport goods from bus stations to taxi ranks for movement across the city. Finally, head porters escort browsing shoppers and relieve them of their purchases to make for unencumbered buying experiences.

Headstrong highlights the processes by which those who live precarious lives within and beyond their marginalization can also guide understanding about difference as a social asset, albeit a fragile and tenuous one. Knowledge production around porters is primarily located in migration studies, childhood studies, and reproductive health. In African migration, scholarship typically focuses on transnational migration to Europe and the United States, the "African brain drain," remittance economies, and the extrajudicial harm of immigration policies on migrant experiences. The attention to domestic migration, which constitutes most of women's migration in Ghana, centers on the surplus labor economies of cities, health inequities, and housing insecurity. Although African youth compose 19 percent of the world's population, and young people are just over half the population in Ghana, most studies on the "amorphous category of youth" frequently extrapolate through heteronormative and androcentric urban lenses (Manful 2022, 473). In contrast, *Headstrong* aims to situate youth through the perspective of the young women and girls who porter, not only as a counter to the constitution of "youth" as a masculine enterprise but also because porters are often the go-to recipients of nongovernmental organization (NGO) programming initiatives, media attention around street children, and public outcry around child labor.

During early independence, when Ghana instituted the Alien Compliance Order of 1969, the state expelled 100,000 foreign nationals, including the

Nigerian men who previously dominated porter work at the market and the indigo trade across the region (Aremu and Ajayi 2014; McKinley 2021). Since then, the number of *kayayei* at work in markets has steadily grown, and porters are now "a ubiquitous part of the vocabulary of Ghanaian markets." In the early 2000s, porters were stigmatized as undesirable street children (GNA 2009). Much of that public discourse revolved around the origin of porters, their living conditions in Accra, and how their labor coalesces as undesirability in urban spaces. The uptick in media coverage about porters over the last twenty years ranges from the half dozen BBC photo stories that feature porters to a Pulitzer Center awardee project and a Fulbright scholar's launch of a daycare facility in Accra.

Public sentiments help explain how gendered work perpetuates patriarchy and also shed light on how women's bodies serve as an oppositional proxy of progress and development. The girls and women who porter are perceived as "out of place" (Opare 2003, 34) because the physical presence of head-loaders and the role they serve as essential laborers may be crucial to market efficiency, but socioeconomic differences also inform ideas about who is entitled to access their rights as an urban inhabitant and about those who "'belong' and those who belong *less*" (Peter Geschiere, quoted in Kobo 2010, 68; emphasis mine). As Gladys Nyarko Ansah et al. astutely observe, "Even though *Kayayei* are typically Ghanaian nationals, they are ethnically and linguistically not nationals in the states (urban markets)" where they work (2017, 51). For example, on March 2, 2017, the minister of finance, Ken Ofori-Attah (speaking on behalf of President Akufo-Addo's campaign promise of widespread tax cuts), announced plans to abolish the "kayayei tax" (Act 896; Acheampong 2017). This tax, initially conceived by the National Democratic Congress party in 2012 as a 1 percent daily income tax on head porters (Bulmuo 2014), was designed to support the maintenance of public toilets and general waste management in the areas where porters lived and worked. However, when the announcement was made in 2017 about the abolition of the tax, it was panned as eliminating a plan that was never executed. But the no-policy policy did not stop Accra residents from making assertions about who can and should be in the city. So instead of enacting an actual policy, throughout 2018, agents of the Accra Metropolitan Assembly (the political and administrative entity that develops, implements, and regulates plans and policies in the city), city officials, and market security personnel cited a

forthcoming *kayayei* tax as an anti-loitering mechanism to preemptively deter porters from soliciting customers on crowded streets.

Affect Modernity and the African Market

Across the Global South and Africa in particular, modernity and modernization are paired as essential components of progressivist development
(Bloom, Miescher, and Manuh 2014). In the genealogy of postcolonial development or the statecraft of early independence in Africa, modernization is a
set of state projects or policies that aim to foster economic growth. The ravages of global capitalism, colonial-outpost capitalism, slavery, and empire
shore up modernization as a programmatic process of transformation from
"traditional to modern forms of governance, production, and social life" (Miescher, Bloom, and Manuh 2014, 3). Modernity, on the other hand, can hold
space as an "aspirational ontology" (Hart 2016, 10), or social enterprise that
allows people to stake claims to cosmopolitanism through behaviors, attitudes, and habits. These acts and attitudes suggest to them, and others, a
desirous way of being and behaving to signal whatever is considered contemporary and modern. In Ghana, as in many places worldwide, modernity
is tied to neoliberal development policies that are enacted across society, from
policy to popular culture, social attitudes, and habits. For instance, in 2005
and 2007, Hajia Alima Mahama, the minister of women and children's affairs,[5] acknowledged that the state offered too few strategies to address the
push/pull factors of rural-to-urban migration but repeatedly specified that
kayayei were a "threat to the national development agenda" (*ADM* 2005). In
the ensuing years, porters protested market treatment through strikes, re-
sisted forced removal, and formed associations to push against the state's divestment in labor protections and well-being (Essel 2009).

In 2021, the NGO Ghana Girl Guides Association launched the "Power in
Her Hand" project to provide vocational crafts, cooking, and dressmaking
training to Accra head porters (Kudoto 2021). The training program, financed
by the Church of Jesus Christ of Latter-Day Saints and conducted by the
JaneSarf Development Organization, included free medical screening for
250 porters. In December 2021, at an event called "Kayayei Dialogue," a
former minister of gender, children, and social protection, Otiko Afisah

Djaba, advocated for "habitable and convenient market structures" to lessen the labor burdens of head porters. Under the theme "Drop the Pan and Pick Up Your Future," Djaba argued that "modernizing the market" would "maximize the potential of head porters to contribute their quota as the country's human resource" (Apawu 2021). With this overture, Djaba suggests that able-bodied porters are on the cusp of becoming efficient and valued laborers because of infrastructural changes rather than acknowledging the capital gains porter labor already facilitated in the first place. Rather than fall into the traps of empowerment and its performative turns exemplified by the NGO-ization of porters' needs, many women discerned Djaba's statement as a sidestep of their ongoing labor demands vis-à-vis claims that porter obsolescence was the mark of promise toward modernization.

At each of Accra's larger markets, I have observed at least three NGOs with regular operations connected to porters or indirectly so as part of their mission statements on at-risk youth and "street child" populations. Some, given their affiliation with Christian churches, advocate abstinence as their only health-safety program, while others acknowledge drug use but do not engage in any programming around safe use or practices.

Most programs cannot be promoted widely since the number of attendees exceeds the availability of resources, and they struggle with sustainability. For example, in 2019, the Kayayoo Empowerment Society held hepatitis B screenings at Tudu Station. Still, access to follow-up services was limited to participants registered with the National Health Insurance Scheme (NHIS). Also, during that event, health workers spoke Ga or Twi, which left porters with limited fluency in those languages excluded from comprehensive explanations of follow-up care. In another example, an organizational subsidiary of Catholic Action for Street Children ran a crèche for porters for about three months. Hawkers and other sidewalk traders with young children expressed dissatisfaction with their exclusion from these services. The possibility of addressing their complaints or expanding services was moot, as the funding for the daycare ended after just one quarter. Familiar with how many NGOs function and the perennial lack of sustainability and institutional longevity for their programming, organizations like Kaya Childcare and Uni-Jay focused on smaller-scale projects like school enrollment for the children of porters and boasted admirable matriculation rates.

Women porters and their work as laborers challenge the virtuous sentiment attached to modernity and their experiences unearth the uneven delivery of its promises. With *Headstrong*, I uncouple modernity from modernization and frame modernity and modernness as a blend of somatic narratives, cultural productions, and state policies that conceive and enact what is felt as contemporary, desirable, and up to date. Modernity in an affective framework examines how the emotion and sensibilities of banal encounters reflect structural inequities in daily life.

Affective relations manifest an assemblage of intimacies, self-making, autonomous acts, and conflict. The physical and emotional intimacies of porters as laborers are an epistolary framework for the habits and practices that speak back to modernness. Modernity as affectual allows ethnography to show the repertoire of histories and patterns that uncover the material consequences and sensory registers of belonging and livelihood (see Hart 2016, 2024; Quayson 2020). Hortense Spillers elegantly demonstrated how, in the plantation economies of the African diaspora, Black women's flesh formed the locus for "converging political and social vectors that mark flesh as a primary commodity of exchange" (1987, 75). With *Headstrong*, I examine how porters' bodies and their labor at the market form an anti-hub of modernness, one that is underwritten by slavery and colonialism. I argue that women porters, and the tensions they represent between body as flesh and body as technology, are fundamental to notions of what it means to be contemporary and present in Accra.

The marginalization of African and diasporic women's intellectual output in these conversations contributes to a perception of Africans as perennial objects, subjected to the gaze and consideration of others. Throughout the book, I draw on African and diasporic scholars to push against the pathological exclusion and marginalization of African and African-descendant scholars in African studies. *Headstrong* is oriented toward African feminism and Black feminism because Black feminist scholars have always examined how lifeworlds and livelihoods exist within broader structures of race, gender, and class. The work feminist scholars have done to uncover how race and racism are part of power hierarchies is especially useful for analysis of African markets—essential spaces for women's work, where women are both hypervisible and disposable. The socioeconomic and regional exclusion porters confront has little to do with how hard they work or the places they live but rather is the result of normalized marginalizations that long precede and predate the decision to come to Accra for work. There are many reasons why women who carry loads of goods on their heads are considered "out of place" in Accra (Opare 2003). Many porters are circular migrants who spend several months or years traveling to and from the city. Even though some women are intergenerational porters, most are not long-term inhabitants of southern Ghana. The women move from agricultural northern regions and often are not fluent in the southern lingua francas (G. N. Ansah et al. 2017). Also, although they work at markets, the primary site of women's labor in Ghana, porters sell their physical labor rather than trade in goods. Finally, porters from regions where polygamy is more open and common are assumed to be Muslim; plural marriage is characterized by urbanites as a provincial foil of "progress" and modernity (Engelke 2010; Meyer 1998, 2008).

Whether in academic theory or daily social life, bell hooks has argued, Black women are perceived as "all body, no mind" (1991, 153), meaning that we are primarily viewed in terms of our physical bodies and sexuality and objectified by what a body represents or does rather than for our intellectual capacities, which are summarily ignored or dismissed. In challenging these reductionist views, hooks concludes that if Black women's names remain unknown or lack a framework for the breadth of their experience, when women push back or disappear, there will be too few tools to name and understand why. That is why *Headstrong* centers the interiority and worldviews women porters have and what they share in moments of leisure, labor, or anger to hold space for this vital set of sensibilities. This approach is also part of the effort for more ethnography to explain *how* African women shape the world around them rather than endure it or be victims of it (Decker and Baderoon 2018). *Headstrong* does not minimize or turn away from the weights of poverty that impinge on the lives of women porters, but the book strives to amplify how women who live within the crosshairs of structural violence do craft sustaining and substantive intimacies in everyday life. *Headstrong* witnesses a map of entanglements and shows how women narrate, surveil, and shade power within fields of near impossibility. As women who grapple with systemic underemployment and marginality, they also imaginatively make do to make sense of the contradictory and complex prescriptivism of their lives. The rules, practices, and conditions that lead someone to migration dictate that the tougher the landscape, the more resourceful the person on the move must be. Migrant girls and women move within the excesses of precarity and do the best they can within fields of probability that are against them in so many ways. At the same time, their minute freedoms exist within exhaustive labor norms. So, too, does the work of Black feminist scholars who illuminate how liberatory moments push against structural violence.

African feminists and African studies and Black studies scholars have done tremendous work to debunk the dichotomies of traditional versus modern that are associated with behavior in Africa. Still, in many ways, *Headstrong* comes into being against strong intellectual headwinds. First, in anthropology, a North Atlantic hegemony exists in the theory and citational practices about modernity (Trouillot 2003; Smith 2015). Second, despite the philosophical overtures and activist orientations toward Africa in Africana and Black studies, there remains a pathological exclusion of Black scholars and scholarship within African studies (Mafeje 1998; Allman 2019). Issues of performative name-dropping of African (and African-descendant) scholars and the marginalization of African scholarship, when considered together, reveal a tendency to reference African and African-descendant scholars without sustained engagement with their work on modernity, race, and blackness, which perpetuates a parochialism that sidelines rather than centers African and African-descendant scholars and their contributions to the field.

Headstrong aims to bring Black studies into closer conversation with the anthropology of Africa by using African and Black feminisms as the theoretical and methodological grounding of the book. Rosabelle Boswell (2017, 193) contends that ethnography tends to be verbocentric, meaning that stories pay closer attention to discursive context than the narrative's embodied affect and sensory politics. By extending Audre Lorde's "the personal is political" to add that the "perceptual is political also," Boswell proposes *sense-work* as a way of listening and writing that links the social orders of gender, race, and class to "visual, gustatory, aural, and olfactory aspects" of bodily experiences and power (196–97). With this, *Headstrong* also unpacks how gender and heteronormativity converge as a platform for antiblackness that tacks poverty and immobility onto the lives of the head porters at Accra's Makola Market. Sense-work is a vantage point that shows how ordinary lives can engage the knotty tangles of modernity in contemporary Ghana. Finally, *Headstrong* resists quantitative data sets or the appendixes to policy recommendations where African women are so often placed and, instead, relies on ethnography of lived experiences and makes women's narratives central in the theories and methods of the book. The book's citational practice also follows the call of African feminists and the Cite Black Women Collective to acknowledge, engage with, and to intentionally cite the expertise of African and African descendant women scholars in theory, method and praxis. (Decker and Baderoon 2018, Smith et. al 2021). Many African girls' and women's lives are imperiled within systems of global white supremacy, antiblackness, and misogynoir and these are not glossed here (Bailey 2021). Still, as a Black feminist ethnography, *Headstrong* uses African women's sense-work as a crucial site of theory making where the stories about why porters migrate, their work in the human transportation sector of Accra, their intimate relationships, and the various places they call home all serve as hermeneutics to illuminate how limited resources are cobbled together with creative persistence.

The Structure of the Book

As the title of this book suggests, *Headstrong* has a polysemous value. First, and most discernibly, it acknowledges the physical puissance required to carry items on one's head for extended periods. Second, as an adjective, *headstrong* describes a person who is not easily restrained or expresses an ungovernable will. To be described as headstrong, for female-identified bodies, is usually to be considered a problem. In most cases, the character attribute implies nonconforming behavior and a need for correction. Still, like the charmingly rebellious Nyasha in Tsitsi Dangarembga's *Nervous Conditions* (1988) or effusive Janie in Zora Neale Hurston's *Their Eyes Were Watching God* (1937), *Headstrong* marks the stubbornness that typifies early adulthood and moves against controls on one's sexuality and body. The word *headstrong* also speaks to my affinity for the transgressive behaviors of unrespectability, with recalcitrant stories that emerge from extended fieldwork and attention to how women buttress the precarities of poverty through relational succor.

Drawn on twenty years of market observations and interactions (1998–2018), continuous fieldwork with sixty porters from 2007 to 2008, including photography-based qualitative interviews and focus groups, follow-up fieldwork in 2015 and 2016, and interviews with traders and market customers during these years, *Headstrong* witnesses how young women contend with, push through, and occasionally *get over on* the consequences of their aspirations and efforts to improve their lives. The title may appear to flirt with the "strong Black woman" stereotype,[6] but the book pays attention to how young women confront the discord of their social location and their cumulative experiences. The book and its title also embrace the untidy knots of ethnography because, even if there are few "wins," people do endeavor to push against malaise. By this, I mean the vigor spurred by a sense of unease or discomfort. Such efforts to at least try are a response to other people's imaginations about who they think porters are, which also traces the residue of coloniality in the present. In the spirit of these converging lineages, *Headstrong* is intentional in its embrace of the ambivalent testimonies of headstrong women.

Most of the chapters of the book open with stories to take a person-first approach to the theory, method, and analysis. (The exception, Chapter 3, begins with an evaluation of photography as a feminist method; more on that below.) The first chapter, "Makola Fires: Old and New," introduces readers to the day-to-day functions of Makola Market, its history, and how porter labor supports transportation and trade at the market. Markets are an essential space for women's work and a place where women are marked as hypervisible and disposable. Markets are also sites of labor extraction, economic accumulation and marginalization, as well as physical exhaustion. Makola Market, one of the few spaces where women do the most work in public outside the house, is where porters sell physical labor rather than trade in goods, and those women do not garner the protofeminist benefits of marketplaces. Instead, porters endure a parasitic city with dispossessive housing norms, pathological harms, and food insecurity (Obeng-Odoom 2010). In the last section of the chapter, I detail how the range of my own personal and professional experiences in Accra informs how and why I introduce readers to women porters through stories and how that history overlaps with changes at Makola Market and Accra over the last twenty years. The chapter closes with details of the requisite study-up women do in order to shift their lives from laboring on family farms to working in the gig economy of head-loading.

Ghana is one of the most studied countries in Africa, yet relative to this strong intellectual focus, too few scholars examine race (Pierre 2012).

Still, the distance between blackness as a global intellectual conversation and enactment of social exclusion and modernity in Ghana is a short one. Class position, gender, and geographic locale are determinants of privilege that supposedly sidestep race and ethnicity in Ghana, but in Chapter 2, "Racial Transcripts of Modernity," I argue that Makola Market, porterage, and the stories of porters constitute an essential site for understanding how racial vernaculars operate in a Black-majority nation-state. Most porters who work at Ghanaian markets are migrants from regions north of the city of Kumasi, including the Northern, Oti, Upper West, Upper East, and parts of the Volta. As a postcolonial outpost and undesirable elsewhere, porters from "the north" and other people from the area, irrespective of their status as citizens, are regularly framed as Others on a "savage slot" range (Trouillout 2003) in the southern Ghanaian imagination. In press coverage and policy, the survival strategies women porters employ are disparaged and stigmatized because, as migrants, they are susceptible to the prejudices of language, locale, and labor. In this chapter I analyze how racial scripts insinuate and imply racial logics in everyday conversation, which I argue exist as narrations of antiblackness. Ordinary encounters reveal how racial transcripts about northern Ghana, which would be easily recognized as discourses on blackness and antiblackness outside of Africa, are instead expressed through metaphors of ethnicity, gender, and class. I argue that modernity, whether statecraft or sensibility, is a nexus of power that refuses certain labor regimes through arrangements about belonging and social entitlement and that porters' lives lay bare what happens after bodies are mechanized and instrumentalized in a surplus service economy. Throughout this chapter, I demonstrate how cardinal direction exceeds geography and that the north-south divides of Ghana are awash with signifiers around blackness. I show how these cues, which appear in policy, practice, and discourse, predate colonization, were institutionalized during the slave trade, and continue today in a variety of development projects and social programs. I also argue that many scholars misrecognize these racial scripts due to the academic focus on ethnicity rather than race, and also because the transatlantic slave trade is more often discussed as a project of the tourism industry than a public memory or historical reckoning. From macrosocial and transnationally attuned policies of return migration to commonly traded insults and class monikers, race and blackness gatekeep processes that assess which bodies are perceived as entitled to employment and accommodation in Accra.

Chapter 3, "Radical Listening and Haptic Sifting," is the methodological center of the book, and it also explains a series of ephemeral encounters to make interior thoughts and emotions more visible and then serve as hermeneutics of social negotiations usually hidden from plain sight. Black feminist anthropologist Faye V. Harrison has pointed out that "there are no feminist methods per se" (2007, 25), but there are methodological orientations that fruitfully court social intimacies and deepen knowledges about care, how it functions, and when it falters (Tamale 2020). I use Rosabelle Boswell's sense-work as a research method alongside photovoice to create a sensory feminist praxis (Bowles 2021). Photovoice is an increasingly popular participatory action research method that uses participants as experts in their own lives (Wang and Burris 1997). At various stages of my fieldwork in Ghana, porters used cameras to document their everyday lives and analyzed the meaning of their pictures. In this chapter I outline how visual projects lead to conversations about trauma and care and difficult experiences not often captured or represented within the frame of an image. I describe this as a sensory feminist praxis because of the affective nature of most of these interactions. Also, in the same way that unfiltered or unprocessed fieldnotes are not shared in full, I focus on the ethnographic outcome of photography as a shared experience instead of using photographs as supplemental to or representational of reality.

As a sensory feminist praxis, photovoice had a critical role in surfacing emotions, serving in what Sara Ahmed (2004) calls an affective economy, one that orients individuals within and in relationship to social spaces and communities. Woven in with stories about evening walks and cooking meals, sensory feminist praxis enlivens ethnographic accounts of African women and ardently refuses objectivity. Of the sixty porters I interviewed throughout my fieldwork in Accra, twelve participated in photography projects. I taught this group how to use 35 mm and digital cameras, which they then used to take pictures and discuss their photos. This approach brings much-needed understanding to the affective aspects of African women's experiences and uses photography practices as a way to engage the interiorities of marginalization and the way women make sense of persistent and unresolved precarity. The multisensory registers accessed in stories about sight, taste, touch, smell, and emotion are intentional in their methodological priority. Conversations archive feelings, and images are a sentient placeholder for ambivalence, anger, joy, disgust, and pleasure. Innocuous and emotionally avoidant stories about attire, food, hair, and rest are critical theorizations of affinities and family, state practice, and corporate enterprise and chart women's plaintive refusal of dominant narratives about who they are and what they do.

Chapter 4, "Queering Polygamy," explores porterage as a flexible wage-earning strategy that subsidizes porters' lives beyond the constraints of compulsory monogamy[7] and heteronormativity. This chapter opens with the story of Tani and Barakesu, co-wives who, following a shared tragedy, organized their circular migration to Accra for work. Their multiple-partner marriage queers polygamy, which is presumed to be a patriarchal output where women have little autonomy. The chapter explores how their habits of reciprocity, pleasure, and work garner greater financial security for their family. Tani and Barakesu refuse the impossibilities often attached to African women's lives and show how families maintain cohesive relationships against corrosions of global capitalism and inequity, adding complexity to the ethnographic excesses of African polygyny as purely gendered oppression.

The autonomy of Black women, particularly African women, and especially those who are economically disadvantaged, is often unrecognized and rarely envisioned as accessible. This chapter argues that Barakesu and Tani's queer polygyny reveals care as generative and oppositional, even as they superficially acquiesce and present as heteronormative. Global capitalism often casts autonomy as a universalist assumption that means the ability to control one's individual choices. However, as Tani, Barakesu, and other women discussed in this chapter assert, autonomy exists within a network of relationships—some that are sensual and sexual, but not always—but is constantly negotiated and reimagined. The poetics of love and homemaking described in this chapter reveal how women buttress head-loading struggles.

Oriented by femme-social intimacies, Chapter 4 unpacks queer autonomies through sensual and sexual behaviors and details how women thrive in their relationships, irrespective of the naming conventions attached to their identities and decisions. Homosocial intimacies refer to close, nonsexual bonds and interactions between individuals of the same sex, and these relationships do not necessarily involve romantic or sexual attraction. Most of the research on homosociality refers to relationships between men.[8] More often, homosocial intimacies between women are feminized and presented as close friendships or best-friend relationships. I use the term *femme-social* in contrast to *homosociality* to acknowledge Black femmes who live at the intersection of blackness and femme identity. Femme sociality expresses a deliberate subversion or exaggeration of patriarchal expectations of femininity (J. M. Johnson 2020). By situating Barakesu and Tani's relationships as both an expression of desire and sustenance for achieving financial autonomy, this chapter shows how women porters broaden ideas of who constitutes a household and how stakeholders in a marriage are organized.

The fifth and final chapter, "Milly, Rastabroni, and a Hothead," serves as the analytical bookend, encapsulating the ethnography's form and content: the less power a woman has in the market, the more creativity she must muster to express displeasure without the threat of violence. Beginning with a disagreement at the market, I examine the significance of nicknames and aliases, as expressed through wage myths and monikers for strangers. As shorthand for social positioning, monikers can code behaviors and attitudes as transgressive or respectful. Pushback against disempowerment, then, must also be clever amelioration of the likelihood of violence. This final ethnographic moment synthesizes the book's central thesis, that the women who work as porters in Accra are crucial figures for expanding our understanding of African life in four areas. First, women's accounts illuminate the epistemic benefit and methodological contributions of African feminisms and Black feminism for ethnography. Second, porters' lives show how ethnography from below unearths the complexities of social programming and development in an African city and how people live inside and beyond the limits to their agency. Third, the book demonstrates how the vectors of power that structure women's lives do not preclude them from actualizing sensibilities of autonomy as laborers, lovers, wives, friends, and mothers. Fourth, gig work, widely understood as an output of the digital age, runs counter to conceptualizations of Africa as in the cusp of the contemporary and innovative. At the same time, the toxic intersections of patriarchy and capitalism are hardly new, and porters exist within accelerated forms of unbelonging. Porterage is a prescient manifestation of the current global gig economy because porters engage in temporary work based on flexible arrangements that are facilitated through technology (carrying pans) and in the service of various clients. Finally, the sociohistorical determinants of head-loading, underwritten by codes of race, place, gender, and class, are particularly pronounced in the context of the subservient occupational identity porter labor holds. Working as a head porter in the market means being, like many gig workers elsewhere, a near anonymous but immediate and anticipatory responder to someone else's needs. In this case, for anyone who utters the word *kayayoo* into the air, a woman will respond to the request. Operating within a sphere of pathological depersonalization, head-loading, like other forms of gig work, demands new kinds of negotiation and creativity to preserve one's humanity and community. This book is a witness to the aspirations and angst of these efforts.

CHAPTER 1

Makola Fires: Old and New

On July 5, 2021, Rosemary, owner of a storeroom near Derby and Thompson Roads, video called me via WhatsApp. As I answered, the phone brought into view billows of smoke darkening the cloudless skies above Makola Market. Rosemary was calling from the second floor of a building half a block away from where a fire was tearing through a three-story building. Plumes of smoke and soot, resembling a movie scene, blanketed the phone's screen. Using her phone to pan the ground below, Rosemary showed how the crowd of witnesses grew along with the flames. Due to the pandemic, passersby wore masks, but as the smoke thickened, people pulled handkerchiefs from their pockets and purses to shield their eyes as they moved away from the burning building. Her voice trembling in a mix of anger and fright, Rosemary said, "A man said fire services had already been [here], but they came with empty water trucks. Can you imagine?" Together, we watched the fire snake the top floors of the building, until a regular phone call came through Rosemary's phone and caused our WhatsApp video to pause.

"Somebody is ringing; lemme call you back," said Rosemary before ending the conversation. Within minutes, photographs of the fire popped up in more WhatsApp chats. I opened my laptop to check *GhanaWeb* and *Citi News* online; on both, breaking news feeds flashed at the top of the banner (*Citi Newsroom* 2021). *Joy News*'s (2021) livestream corroborated Rosemary's claim about the fire services' arrival in waterless trucks; at least a dozen shops were ablaze inside the Hong Kong building.

When she called back a few minutes later, Rosemary used her phone to pan the skyline behind Kwame Nkrumah Avenue. The fire had spread to adjoining multistoried buildings. Traders streamed out of the buildings, some holding cash drawers or goods as they fled. People threw bags of money out of shop windows to save the paper. Thick plumes of ash puffed above orange flames. On the street in front of the building, people sobbed, their bodies sagging with agony and distress. Livelihoods burned quickly, and traders cried as inventory curled in the flames. Rosemary shrieked and the phone shook as we watched three people hold a man back as he attempted to run back into his store. The man owned an electronics shop. Rosemary speculated that he must have just received a shipment because they normally arrive at the start of each month.

People walked to the Tudu Fire Service Station to express rage after more than an hour passed without signs of the fire service's return. Later in the day, Ellis Robinson Okoe, head of public relations at Ghana National Fire Service, said the service's initial efforts to douse the flames were thwarted because of the low water pressure in the fire hydrants of the central business district, which left firefighters having to port water from elsewhere (*GhanaWeb TV* 2021). I was still on the line with Rosemary when the fire trucks did return to Kwame Nkrumah Avenue. A notification pop-up on WhatsApp announced Rosemary's low phone battery, its dwindling energy mirroring the weariness etched in her voice. Noticing her tiredness, one of her storeroom staffers offered to stay in town and keep Rosemary abreast of what was going on. Thankful for the offer and utterly exhausted, Rosemary exchanged goodbyes with me, ended the call, and headed home.

WhatsApp chats with other people narrated the next seven hours it took to quell the fire. Eyewitnesses levied harsh criticisms against the fire services, no matter Okoe's claims about water access. For several days, the Makola fire and the subsequent blame on the fire services, the Accra Metropolitan Assembly (AMA), and the government were the lead stories on *Joy News* and *Citi News*. After the fire headlined national TV and radio news, friends who lived as far as Cape Coast and Kumasi sent news stories via chat. By the next day, July 6, the police had cordoned off the fire area. Until July 10, the AMA placed patrollers to guard the area against people entering the remains of the building. Mid-month, young people who worked in the nearby scrap metal processing sites began to forage the rubble. A month passed before the

48 Engineer Regiment of the Ghana Armed Forces, the AMA, and the Allied Agencies of Ghana began the demolition on the three burned-out buildings. It took three weeks to fully dismantle them. Once demolition no longer required the heavy machinery of cranes, piles of rubble were organized in the gaping space where the buildings once stood.

When I texted Zaynab about the fire, she expressed certainty that the buildings were unsalvageable. She also speculated that porters would do the lion's share of rubble removal. The buildings were privately owned, so after the demolition and removal of the major debris, the space would return to the control of the owner. By October, sandy dust piles remained of the Hong Kong building. Zaynab and Rosemary confirmed that for a few hours each day, hired porters used their pans to load the remaining dust and stones to trucks headed for a quarry.[1] They were told that the rocky debris was to be pulverized and remixed to make cement blocks. Zaynab heard a rumor that several trucks were seen dumping the rubbish on the beach as part of an ad-hoc effort to mitigate coastal erosion.

In their reports to Zaynab, porters shared that they earned one cedi for each completed load from rubble to truck, with the truck driver peeling a single red one-cedi note from a stack after each pan was emptied into the dump box. Each hour of work, then, earned a porter about two cedis (US$0.15). At the per-task rate they were paid, rather than a daily wage, the work was excessively demanding; it was too burdensome for women to endure a full eight to twelve hours of hauling construction material. This was compounded by the lack of protective gear, as the women were hoisting heavy stones and concrete pieces. The returns from this labor were minimal; with no protective gear and scooping with bare hands, no one dedicated more than an hour to the job. They only engaged in the work when there was a lull in load work elsewhere at the market.

In 2021, the state-mandated minimum daily wage in Ghana was GH₵12.53 (US$1.77).[2] But it is uncommon for porters to be hired for an entire day of work. More commonly, the hirer, like the truck driver mentioned above, estimates the duration of a job and compensates porters on a per-trip basis. Similarly, when traders move merchandise throughout the market, whether they are distributing bulk goods to vendors or closing their stall and store at the end of the business day, the cost of employing head-loaders is seldom factored into overhead (Clark 1994). Instead, porters are usually paid from whatever pocket change the hirer possesses.

*   *   *

Fire is not new for Makola Market. In fact, in colloquial Ga, the expression "Ma ko la" means "I am going for fire" (Darkwah 2007, 64), a phrase used by women in the area to refer to collecting hot coals from neighborhood Hausa kebab sellers as a convenient shortcut for sparking a cooking fire. Originally consisting of state-sanctioned council stalls and an adjacent sales area, today Makola Market is a discontinuous cluster of markets that house a plethora of sidewalk sale areas in the central business district of Accra. Women's trade in West Africa dates to the seventeenth century, but the androcentric observations of early anthropologists and missionaries, saturated with Victorian attitudes about womanhood, frequently missed the gendered, classed, and ethnic differences of precolonial trade norms (Akyeampong and Fofack 2014). The bend of British imperialism strongly influenced how markets function in Ghana today, reflecting an ethos that favored men as primary breadwinners, considered men the financial stalwarts of a household, and institutionalized male ownership of land (Allman 1996). As a result, clerical and civil servant positions were afforded exclusively to men, leaving the market as the rare economic niche for women to work within (Oyewùmí 2003). After World War I, the British built a rail line between Kumasi and Accra to expedite the expropriation of cocoa from the Gold Coast. In 1924, the Accra Town Council constructed a building to operate as a market site at the railroad with permanent stalls to streamline taxation and colonial surveillance of traders' pricing strategies (Chamlee-Wright 2002). The one-story building became known as Makola Market No. 1.

A short walking distance from the beaches of the Atlantic, behind the Supreme Court, and just north of Kwame Nkrumah Memorial Park, market trade dominates the commercial sector of Accra's business district. The whole area is casually referred to as Makola, but it also includes the secondhand clothing market Kantamanto, affectionately called "Bend Down Boutique" because garments are organized in heaps that one must bend over to browse, which abuts Agbogbloshie Market, which has some of the freshest produce for sale in the city. Brisk trade is always underway at the Tema and Tudu bus stations (also called TS), where hawkers stroll between the lanes of parked minibuses awaiting departure. Okaishie Market stretches from Derby Avenue to Kinbu Gardens and Rawlings Park, the pedestrian square located between Market Street, Derby Avenue, and Kojo Thompson Road.

The official Makola Market Nos. 1 and 2 operate between Barnes and Kojo Thompson Roads. These are not their original homes. The Makola Market No. 1 that was built in the 1920s is now a four-block rectangular pedestrian commercial space. The space colloquially known as Rawlings Park, Rawlings Square, or JJ Park houses a parking lot and a taxi rank and serves as a pedestrian-friendly thoroughfare between heavily congested market streets. In 1979, soldiers in the Armed Forces Revolutionary Council (AFRC), led by Flight Lieutenant John Jerry Rawlings, destroyed the original Makola Market No. 1. A story often told by market elders is that "during JJ's time" women traders refused to make "special prices" for soldiers in a time of growing food insecurity. When soldiers aggressively insisted on reduced prices, market women responded by peeing on the ground to assert their refusal. Following this affront, soldiers accused Makola traders of hoarding market goods and driving up demand and prices.

In reality, agricultural production had declined due to inflation (Robertson 1983). Still, the AFRC soldiers burned Makola to the ground to "teach Ghanaian women to stop being wicked" (Bentsi-Enchill 1979, 1592). The AFRC claimed that the market was destroyed as a response to the *kalabule* (corruption) of women traders, who undermined military plans to construct a "modern private parking lot" at the site after the first demolition (Fraker and Harrell-Bond 1979). Trade resumed after the 1979 destruction, but Makola was razed by the Rawlings regime again in 1981, which was followed by the construction of a parking lot and children's playground.

Today, the only things that remain of the children's playground are the rusted coil bases for spring riders and the remnants of a seesaw. Near the center of the park is a towering stone catenary arch reminiscent of the Gateway Arch in St. Louis, Missouri, or the Hiroshima Peace Memorial in Japan. The market demolition and subsequent monumental arch is an example of "modernization as spectacle," a multilayered process of modernization with institutional and social effect (Miescher, Bloom, and Manuh 2014, 1). The Rawlings arch exemplifies regime power through an imposing monument that is a placeholder and memorialization of state violence against women traders and compounds the colonial binds that tied market women to anti-virtuousness and regressions of progress. And now, each day, vegetable sellers and other traders strategically lay their sale mats so that much of their day is spent in the shade of the looming arch.

By the time I began fieldwork for my anthropology dissertation, I'd been traveling to Accra for nine years. In 1998, I studied at the University of Ghana, the largest university in the country, located in Legon, Accra, in the suburbs of the city. In that undergraduate cohort of thirty-five students, colleges and universities from across the United States were represented. Six of us, including four Black women on a natural-hair-care journey with shared music taste in reggae and hip-hop, forged a lifelong friendship fomented by a collective embrace of the entire city as part of our study abroad experience. New friendships bloomed with DJs and radio presenters at Vibe and Groove FM, and we dove headfirst into the bourgeoning hip-hop, hiplife, and reggae scene of the city. Nearly every day after class, we traipsed around town to music performances and the hottest nightclubs and sought vegetarian-friendly restaurants. One night, while at reggae night at Paradise Club in the Osu neighborhood, we learned about Jah Rah, a vegetarian spot in the heart of Makola Market. With that bit of information, coupled with the rumor that Makola Market was where the most affordable fabric in town could be found, my friends and I made our way from the university campus to the central business district.

Camouflage was and continues to be banned as civilian attire in Ghana, but blue-and-brown camouflage hats fashioned after the iconic Che Guevara military image were all the rage. I learned from (then) up-and-coming hiplife artist Reggie Rockstone that the fabric could be bought at Makola Market and made into a Che hat by a sewist in his neighborhood. On our program-sponsored group tour of Makola, a student in our cohort was pickpocketed at the market, which had soured most of our classmates on that part of town. Still, these new bits of information about shopping and vegetarian food increased my squad's determination to venture from Legon. By 2000, when my friends and I reunited in Accra to celebrate our undergraduate graduations, we lived in the Osu neighborhood, closer to High Street, and visited the city center regularly. In 2003, we reconvened again in Accra and spent the summer celebrating the start or end of graduate school for each of us.

These early visits to Accra are part of my coming-of-age experience and deepened my affinity for Accra, a penchant for cities in general, and my attention to how women take up space in urban areas. As a fourth-generation Philadelphian whose identity is rooted by a great-grandmother two generations survived from enslavement in South Carolina, I remain curious about the interplay between infrastructure and interiority and how structures of feeling shape labor sensibilities and belonging. I am ever fascinated about who is entitled to take up space in certain places, how forms of inclusion also work to police exclusion, and how unbelonging becomes known and embodied.

From 2008 to 2019, I spent most of my time conducting fieldwork about porters with women who porter in and around the east side of the square, closest to Makola Circle. Just in front of Makola Circle is a monument to the Ga Mantse Tackie Tawiah III. The rectangular square is enclosed by stone walls and wrought-iron fencing, where traders display goods, most often cookware, utensils, and food-storage items, on the tall outer walls. The western exit of the park is a pedestrian-only sidewalk, while opposite it is the entrance and exit for a privately owned parking lot and taxi rank.

In the center of the park, there are usually a dozen large delivery trucks, which arrive at dawn to load or unload bulk goods heading to and from nearby warehouses. Because of this, porters who work in this area have steady work most mornings, loading and unloading trucks. Some delivery drivers have unloading budgets, but others are expected to pay porters from their fuel allotment for the trip, which leaves a range of uncertainty around what the wages for the work will be until the tasks are completed.

The ethnic enclaves and dispersals of women porters at Makola mirror labor distributions in Ghana and West Africa more broadly.[3] Ethnicity overlaps with who engages in what kinds of labor or trade at the market, which is not unique to Makola or the city, nor is it exclusively tied to porters or African people. For readers unfamiliar with Accra, maps may seem instructive to help conceptualize and imagine Makola, and the city, but that approach runs the risk of reinscribing the primordialism attached to ethnicity that *Headstrong* strives to write against. Also, the existing maps of Makola Market are based on colonial renderings, which I am hesitant to reproduce, especially given the way the clusters of laborers at Makola Market are in flux. For instance, during my fieldwork year of 2007–8, the women porters around Rawlings Park ethnically self-identified as Konkomba or Grunshie, while a high concentration of porters at Tudu Station called themselves Mamprusi or Dagbana. In subsequent fieldwork visits in 2014 and 2016, these ethnicized labor enclaves had shifted. Near Tema Station, most of the porters I interviewed and interacted with were Nanumba- and Mossi-identified women and girls. Therefore, in a multiethnic nation-state with centuries of domestic migration, it is useful to consider ethnicity as a discursive tool that also marks class, mobility, and racialism rather than to outline ethnic enclaves in a cartographic sense.

In addition to ethnicity, religion and region also structure the labor clusters for work around the market. Many people assume women porters are Muslim because they cover their hair during head-loading work. Many porters do come from Islamic households, but even porters who are Christian or practitioners of indigenous religions dress modestly, in long skirts, knee socks, or hair covering to protect their skin from sunburn and dust.

*   *   *

Accra's year-round warmth belies the challenges of shelter that housing-insecure people face each day. Waves of heat rise from sandy paths, and long, slender branches of an acacia tree do carry a breeze across the rubicund earth. During the rainy season, the sun plays peek-a-boo behind slivers of clouds to tease more rain. After hours of hefting and hauling goods and foods throughout the market,[4] many porters must then do the work of finding a place to rest and sleep for the night. To prepare for a night's sleep, whether in a lean-to, kiosk, or emptied shipping container, women place cardboard on the ground first, to mitigate the discomfort of stones or rocky debris. Next to be laid are dried fiber mats and maybe a few bright-colored prayer mats recently arrived from Asian markets. Feet and legs are dusty from flip-flopped kickback on unpaved roads, but the home training of removing shoes when indoors means a mound of footwear is often on the threshold when people do sleep indoors. At some point during every day, someone's baby naps inside the space. Even in the rainy season, when schoolchildren wear puffy vests and sweaters, temperatures in Accra rarely, if ever, dip below seventy-five degrees.

Lean-tos and containers with windows give limited passage to cool air and wide berth to mosquitoes. At night the space might cool to eighty degrees, but thick humidity makes the space much warmer. Inside a container, discarded cardboard drums and wooden pallets store personal items. Some sleeping spaces are metal containers, but most are wooden structures of hammered planks of doors and walls. The blistering slats allow streaks of sun and misty rain to squeeze through, which heightens the mold and offal smells that seep into the room along with neighborhood chatter.

Hasena's baby slept atop a heap of cloth. Outside the swung-open door of the metal lean-to, two toddlers expended creative energies scratching sticks across the ground. Ibrahim flung bottle caps into the mound of black plastic bags that swirled in the detritus of more rubbish. The heavy metal doors of the lean-to sat wide open until bedtime, but not much air circulated through the ten-by-ten-foot shelter. Hasena—in her late twenties, with permed brown hair tucked under a black mesh scarf—wore a loose red T-shirt printed with the cursive Coca-Cola logo over a black pencil skirt that fell below her knees. A yard of cloth, coiled into a circle cushioned the top of her head against the weight of her pan, would turn into a shawl when she was not head-carrying. Her deep contralto voice belies her small stature. When calling for someone over the market din, her silky tone rises to a soprano. Hasena might be considered stern because of the richness of her voice and the curtness of her manner, but her general disposition reflects the seriousness with which she comports herself when she is at work at the market. She enjoys our conversation to be in pidgin English, which she learned from a boyfriend. Pidgin makes use of the English classes she had in her formative years and helps her to situate herself as a bit of a hipster. Solomon, my assistant, is more inclined to linguistic prescriptivism, so he usually refrains from much of those conversations.

During most of her Makola workday, Hasena stationed herself close to the parking attendants at Rawlings Park. On the days she porters elsewhere, she perches herself between a row of shops with busy foot traffic in hopes that customers and shopkeepers will provide a steady stream of work. Hasena sat atop her pan to surreptitiously watch a Nigerian film playing at one of the shops situated between Old Fadama Police Station and the Accra night market. Hasena porters for all the stores on the row, each one specializing in bulk goods like water sachets or wholesale ramen boxes that require pedestrian carriage. The staggered comings and goings of market goods and customers at the wooden boxed stores make the pace of work either frenetic or motionless. Cardboard and corrugated aluminum roof the ten-by-ten wooden slats, and the DVD playing the movie sits atop a box television near the front of the space. Along with a single string of light bulbs, the TV and DVD player are plugged into a power strip with a cord that snakes from the back of the lean-to and down a cinnamon dirt path before disappearing through the window of a another shed-turned-store. With one eye toward shoppers at the various stalls, Hasena watched the wildly popular Nigerian film *Jenifa*. Released in 2008, the comedy chronicles the social miscues of a young "village girl," Suliat, as she strives to learn Lagosian social dictates. For months after its release, *Jenifa* played in the background at neighborhood drinking spots and small shops. The Yoruba-language Nigerian movie became the prequel to the television series *Jenifa's Diary* and a 2019 spin-off, *Aiyetoro Town*.

The movie opens with Suliat (Funke Akindele) confidently walking down the streets of Lagos dressed in a floral romper and white kitten-heel boots. Answering her ringing phone, Suliat has light banter with her parents, who are pleased by her safe arrival at university. Strolling onto campus, Suliat introduces herself to two co-eds, which sets the stage for a series of miscues of the "village girl" just arrived in the metropolis. The women snicker when Suliat answers their queries about her major with "Yoruba studies." The side-eye between the two women is a joke about the lack of seriousness or worthiness of such a course of study. One of the women then suggests they all exchange telephone numbers, but when Suliat hands over her dated flip phone for one of them to enter their mobile number, the woman shrinks back and refuses to hold it. The woman then gives Suliat her dorm room number rather than take the phone from Suliat's outstretched hand.

"Mtchewwwww."

This long hiss and teeth-sucking sound, made by women throughout the African diaspora, marks annoyance. Hasena, engrossed in the movie, pitched her hip toward one of the curved edges of her pan. Hasena does not speak Yoruba or read the English subtitles, but the scene drips with an easily discerned shadiness. As the scene closes and Suliat walks out of the frame, one of the characters turns to the other and asks, "What pajamas with boots is this girl wearing?" Hasena's eyes furrowed and lips pursed. Her approving gaze of Suliat's self-possession gave way to agitation at the ridicule of Suliat's style and accent. I smirked at the mean-girl tone of the scene, which, like Hasena, I was catching a bit of while strolling in the city. Over several months, the popular movie was the background entertainment at lunch spots and chill venues before the nighttime shift to loud music from bass-filled sound systems. Like Hasena and the shopkeeper, I caught bits of the comedy in between other goings-on of the market.

Hasena and so many porters understand their own movement in Accra as a dichotomous contrast bearing strong resemblance to the Suliat character they enjoyed watching. Fuako, Hasena's friend who first accompanied her to Accra when they were barely teens, wore a too-big men's button-down shirt, with the sleeves rolled to her elbows to the invite air to graze her skin when a breeze graced the open space. Fuako's dark-brown skin always glows with a sheen on the cusp of perspiration. Although Fuako was in her early twenties, the corners of her eyes were dressed in wrinkles from her frequent squinting. She is farsighted. Fuako recognizes a person at a distance, but at close range her vision blurs. She used the color differences of cedi notes to count money. The pair were neighbors from a village in the Savannah Region, near Damango. For the last ten years, they have timed their circular migrations to coincide, and they always share accommodations in the city.

As she talked, Fuako rocked from side to side, shifting her weight from one leg to the other, and her *chale wote* squeaked softly in response to her body movement and the lingering moisture of earlier rainfall.[5] In my conversation with Hasena and Fuako, the main character, *Suliat,* is a metaphor for the way people in Accra make them feel like strangers. As we talk about the film, they are also describing the exclusions sutured to their own social encounters, the emotional wedge of their precarity, and their general annoyance toward people who talk badly about porters. Like Suliat, Hasena and Fuako left the village with the hope of earning money to help support the household needs and the supplemental fees of the free government school. Their friends migrated with their toddlers because the children are too young to be useful during harvests. Some of the unmarried girls came to porter to build their wedding trousseaux.

Most days, the number of porters at work in Makola far exceeds the demand for their services. Porters sell labor rather than goods, which means the job has a low overheard, but the physical burdens of head-loading make

it difficult to assess how to earn money worth their time. Women who engage in sex work to supplement their porter wages face the added vilification
of being seen as morally bankrupt. Ajara is a married, twenty-something
mother of two who has spent two and a half years in Accra. She has not returned to her hometown and has no plans to visit. She also has an infant son,
Adamu. Adamu's father is also from a town just west of Yendi. He spends his
workday hawking onions at the vegetable market between Old Fadama and
Agbogbloshie. On evenings when he is not too tired, Adamu's dad brings
Ajara her favorite produce, oranges and overripe plantain. He cuddles and
coos with Adamu. Because she has two children with her in the city, Ajara
sometimes takes her eldest to the crèche run by the NGO Catholic Action
for Street Children for a few hours each day. She hopes Kayayee Youth
Organization will still be operating once the eldest is school-aged because
the aid workers talk about plans to open a free school specifically for porters'
children.

Earlier in the year, Ajara's husband, some three hundred miles away, sent
word that he needed her to come harvest groundnuts on the farm. Farming
provides the nutritional mainstay for the entire country, but the "village" is
considered plagued with parochialism. Ajara's husband waits inside her silence and her decision not to introduce the newborn to the "home family"
while in Accra with her "here people." The prolonged precarity that brought
Ajara to Accra in the first place is now ladened with a complicated and creative autonomy, two long-term relationships, two households, and two
children.

The proliferating global service economy, rife with underemployment and
displacement, makes Ajara and other porters an unexceptional class of surplus laborers and the complexities of their efforts to survive frightfully common. Securing a livelihood in the current global economy is no mean feat
when an overabundance of produce sellers might crowd a single block and
there are taxi ranks on every patch of dirt road surrounding high streets. Carrying pans are a ubiquitous commodity, and porters are the essential laborers of pedestrian-only spaces who shore up the stings of downward mobility
but also highlight the centrality of care communities, networks of sociality,
and reciprocity that are required to bear the labor of survival.

CHAPTER 2

Racial Transcripts of Modernity

When I was an adjunct lecturer in graduate school, my favorite class to teach was an introductory cultural anthropology course, because each semester the class filled with adult learners eager to complete the general requirements toward their bachelor's degrees. As in most first-day-of-class activities, I led the group in icebreakers. While everyone introduced themselves, I took inventory of the space; there was gender parity in the group, I was probably the youngest person in the room, and everyone appeared to be white, except me and one male student. When it was his turn to introduce himself, I grinned when I heard the Ghanaian English inflections in his voice.

"Hi, my name is Steven. I am from a small country in Africa that you have never heard of."

"Try me," I said.

"It's in West Africa. My country is called Ghana. Not Guyana. Ghana." I smiled at Steven's preemptive correction of the common conflation of Ghana with the South American country. I responded, "I know Ghana pretty well."

Steven looked surprised. "You're joking."

"I'm serious. Where in Ghana are you from?" I asked.

"The north."

"Where in the north?" I asked.

"Oh, you are asking me where, so maybe you really know the place. A town near Tamale close to Tugu."

"I don't know Tugu exactly, but I've been to Tamale a few times. I like the pace of the place."

I moved to the next student, finished our introductions, and began the three-hour class in earnest. When we came to the break, Steven and a couple of students chatted in the hallway next to a vending machine. We made small talk as I bought water. Steven asked, "So where do you stay in Ghana?"

"Mostly in Accra and also Cape Coast."

Steven nodded and said, "The south is very different. Those places, they are very special."

"Special how?" I asked.

"Well," he said, "while we northerners were still swinging in the bush, the people down there were schooling, reading, and writing. They were lucky to have the British come."

Taken aback by Steven's logic, I replied, "I think it's a bit more complicated than that." He shook his head emphatically and added, "They brought schools, they built the roads, and they brought the English [language]. And if they had stayed a bit longer, these things would have reached us in the north." I struggled to find my words, thinking, "Damn, it's only the first day."

I had anticipated some pedagogical challenges as the youngest person in the classroom, who was also the professor, who was also a Black woman professor. But I did not expect needing a quip for meso-aggressive comments from a Black person while being watched by some of the nearby white students. With too many layers in the moment that needed to be unpacked, I glanced at my watch and blandly responded, "Well, I look forward to having a lot more conversations like this . . . in class." The pause between the sentences had an authoritative tone, and the group of students responded by moving toward the classroom door. Having sidestepped an increasingly awkward moment, I was relieved the break was over.

The resemblance between Steven's comments and so many conversations among Black people in Africa and the diaspora affirms progressivist notions of infrastructure and development toward places that survived colonialism. By progressivist, I mean the belief that the colonial investments that facilitated extraction are synonymous with public good, progress, essential ingredients of a modern nation-state.

While no singular or continuous space constitutes "the north" in Ghana, there are places, sites, and habits that bind primitivist notions to the unequitable material conditions people from these areas may experience (Holsey 2013). In *Lose Your Mother: A Journey Along the Atlantic Slave Route*, Black studies and literary scholar Saidiya Hartman observes how Accra inhabitants mark the "north-south divide along the lines of brawn versus intelligence" and describe northern Ghana as "the land of barbarians...just stumbled out of caves" who have "the stench of the untamed" (2008, 113). "The north," then is no innocuous cardinal direction or name for a region and its people but a common parlance that collapses ethnicity, class, language, religious affiliation, and geography into a stigmatized and amorphous difference. Steven's own reference to British colonization normalized extractive brutality as a compulsory growing pain for a nation. In this portrayal, "development" is a valiant and desirous turn away from "the bush" and whatever lies there. My discomfort over Steven's colonial sentimentality in front of white people is what Simone Browne describes of surveillance as a "discursive and material practice" (2015, 3), because those listening in, I believe, heard the rehearsal of a well-worn perspective, that colonialism did some good in Africa. Here, Steven rejected the premise that colonialism disrupted modernity in Africa (Táíwò 2010) and instead aligned with colonial development as the primary ingredient of progress. The colonial divestment in infrastructure that did not facilitate capital extraction, and European accumulation becomes a minor character in the march toward modernity (Kambala 2022). The formation of colonial schools as making space for Ghana to become modern is a well-worn and often-trotted-out belief of "common sense." And, while race was not pointedly mentioned, Steven's analogy of the bush invoked idleness and an acephalous elsewhere, through the simian referent of northerners "swinging in the bush," steeped in racist anthropomorphism. Finally, the surveillance and witness of non-Black people to the exchange added to its knottiness and led me to end the conversation prematurely.

During my office hours, later in the semester, Steven and I had many lively conversations about a variety of topics, including reflections on our first day of class together. Steven was excited that there was someone in the space who knew something about Ghana, surprised that I did not argue against his provocations, and later shocked by his own realization that our class was his first encounter in a predominately white educational space. I shared that, despite being the instructor and authority in the classroom, I was unwilling to push back on Steven in front of a group of white people, especially as a non-Ghanaian in front of people with so little knowledge about Africa. This led to a shared lamentation about the challenges of Black solidarity across cultural context and cultivating a shared value for private exchanges about race between Black people. By the end of the semester, Steven and I covered an array of topics during office hours, mostly centered on racial politics, the continuities and discontinuities of blackness, and our favorite Ghanaian dishes.

While this recap of an introductory conversation with a student may be dismissed as anecdote rather than ethnographic data, it is useful for exhibiting a petite legitimatization of coloniality and its underlying racial logics. The framework of the Black body as a problem unfolds in an African context with becoming "special" occurring vis-à-vis proximity to colonial power. This sentiment relegates blackness, Black people, their bodies, as well as their labor, to dehumanized subjects whose value hinges on colonial modernity as a mark of progress.

Nigerian historian Moses Ochonu (2019b) warns that "to advance the social consequences of racialization—the process of constructing, appropriating, and recalibrating racial and neo-racial meanings and giving them utilitarian social valence—is to risk being accused of mistaking other forms of social difference—class, ethnicity, culture—as racial manifestations." In this chapter, I take the intellectual risk Ochonu warns against to demonstrate how modernity and its metaphor modernness are a cloak for socializations of blackness in the everyday lives of Ghanaians (Pierre 2012). Ochonu (2019b) suggests, "Instead of fixating on race as a relational phenomenon forged only in the crucible of interracial interactions," scholars could consider how blackness is "subtle, invidious, banal, and disguised" precisely because it functions in a majority-Black nation-state. Attendance to the ordinary and quotidian patterns and habits not only sidesteps the tired beliefs that "ethnic conflict" or "tribal warfare" are efficient frameworks for understanding conflict in Africa but also rejects the (largely white) scholarly avoidance of race as a useful discernment of power relationships and agency among African people (Mullings 2008, Hagan 2019).

Within discourse on blackness, Ghana is often heralded as an admirable democratic African state, a place of warm welcome and refuge for Black expats and an instrumental site of diasporic heritage. However, these consanguinities of blackness in the spirit of Pan-Africanism or a filial African diaspora cannot diminish our scholarly commitment to understanding the explicit as well as tacit ways that belonging and unbelonging are connected to how modernness is made legible in Accra. In this chapter, I am less invested and interested in illuminating race as embodied through blackness as phenotype; instead, I am committed to demonstrating how blackness functions as a currency that marks who does and does not have access to claims of belonging in Accra; how those sensibilities unfold in rehearsals of modernity, through constant socializations and improvisations around modernness.

Northernness, Modernness, Antiblackness

Used to form abstract nouns from adjectives and other parts of speech, the suffix -*ness* is a generative and versatile element in the English language. When following the root word, -*ness* denotes a state, condition, or quality, or represents an instance of one of these features. The descriptor transforms theoretics about the material into discourses of the affective, somatic, sensible, and sensory. It has long served a role in academic concepts—for example, *otherness* and *consciousness*—because the simplicity and flexibility of -*ness* lies in its ability to make visible how abstract ideas shape up in actual behaviors and attitudes.

Throughout this chapter, I use-*ness* as a conceptual framework in three ways: northernness, modernness, and antiblackness, to focus on place, identity, and sentiment as qualities, attitudes, and conditions in the lives of women who porter and of Ghanaians more broadly. Terms formed with the suffix -*ness* show how people imagine and reimagine their place in the world and creatively render their personal politics. Imagination is revealed in attitudes, actions, performance, and conversation, and relationality valorizes those interconnections and opacity. Words formed with -*ness* refuse transparency and denotative meaning, so I rely on *northernness* to move away from specificities of location and emplace attitudes and ideas as instructive geographies. I use *modernness* to sidestep the androcentric historicisms of *modernity* in order to attend to the sentiments and qualitative aspects of being and being perceived of as up-to-date; a wildly personal and politically oriented feeling about belonging. *Modernness* lends itself to the abstract and ephemeral aspects of these processes and lays bare its day to day consequences and harm. I argue that the sense-work of navigating being a northerner in a southern city illuminates how the material impacts of what is believed to be modern work through discursive gatekeeping about blackness as an ongoing mediation. Finally, racialization shows up in the affective contours of blackness, which moves within and beyond conceptualizations of antiblackness as racism against Black people. I choose *antiblackness* rather than *anti-Black racism* or the hyphenated *anti-blackness* because I want to signal the sense-work of hostility and violence that is aimed toward Black people[1]—specifically, the somatic, performative, and embodied devaluations of Black people and their aliveness, livelihood, and being (Quashie 2012). In this way, antiblackness is also how marginality becomes normalized as proximity to harm or operationalized through daily precarity (Smith 2016). In taking account of antiblackness as affectual, I return, as Black studies scholars have done, to the body as method in order to gather data on the habits and techniques Black people deploy to endure and survive structures of disposability and cumulative dispossession (Mullings 2008).

Throughout this chapter, I argue that "the north" and "northernness," mentioned in interviews as well as day-to-day conversations, can be understood as forms of antiblackness cloaked in characterizations of regional difference. I also suggest that the quotidian commentaries about the north and northerners that take place in Accra, about attitudes, disposition, and character traits, are anxious sense-works around what constitutes a modern African city and constitutes the social currency of blackness as well as its limitations as an index of the contemporary. In conversation with criticisms of the long-standing deployment of African and African-descendant people as the foil for modern constructions of race within and beyond the nation-state (Beliso-De Jesús and Pierre 2019), I consider how antiblackness, as mapped onto the bodies of porters and other rural laborers at work in the city, offers an ethnographic contrast to the regularized inattention to racial projects in an African context (excluding South Africa) (Pierre 2019, 2020). Ethnography can describe the feel and experience of modernity and locates how policy or legacies become routine sentiment. This interplay between the affectual and material qualities of blackness helps explain how progress is understood in daily life, especially when modernity is widely viewed as a recovery from colonialism, an embrace of liberalism, and an orderly and ordered society (Hart 2024). In this chapter I position modernity, or, more aptly, modernness (which aligns with my investment in showing what suffixes can conceptually offer), as a relational temporality in everyday life. First, I focus on some of the ways race is conflated with ethnicity and how that conflation is codified in early anthropological accounts of northern Ghana as well as precolonial and colonial discourse about slavery. Second, I explain how diasporic tourism, as contemporary statecraft, attempts to capitalize on the contradiction and tensions of blackness to artfully nest economic enterprise within filial tropes. Finally, following the work of scholars who have argued for a broad understanding of modernity as dialogic, uneven, multifocal, and historically situated, I describe blackness and modernness as co-constituted on a spectrum of order to untangle when and how negotiations of Black identity are part of modernity as a state project, performative actions, and interpersonal encounter. I aim to demonstrate how. Just as there are politics of respectability, there are politics of modernness and blackness that shape behaviors from the micro- to macrosocial level and range, from the *drylongso* to statecraft.[2]

"The North" as a Racial Palimpsest

The socioeconomic disparities between the Northern, Upper East, and Upper West Regions of Ghana in comparison to southern and coastal regions have been well documented (Songsore 1989; Tsikata and Seini 2004).[3] The long association of Accra and southern Ghana with modernity and cosmopolitanism is not happenstance, nor are the politics that link vocational agriculturalism, such as the family farming of the north, with poverty. The north is the agricultural breadbasket, supplying 90 percent of the country's consumption in cereal, rice, maize, and yams (FAO n.d.), yet infrastructural neglect persists in electricity and education projects (Mohammed 2020). Progressivist perspectives about what constituted development, as well as who shoulders the rights and responsibility to distribute resources, have a long historical arc toward the south of the country. The social dispossession of the north is a legacy of a colonial understanding of chieftaincy, whereby groups with chiefs were legitimated as having the centralized authority capable of allocation of state resources (Wiemers 2015). Modernness, then, as a social project, allows the stigmatization of the north and northerners as signifiers for places that are not up to date and decidedly not cosmopolitan, which is not only false but also fails to account for the legacies of slavery and colonization embedded in today's statecraft.

A strong body of scholarship traces and troubles the dichotomies of north-south development in terms of quality of life (Goody 1995; Lentz 2006; Plange 1979). The designation of regions was a colonial enterprise that codified precolonial stratification with the British self-interest of distinctions between the Gold Coast, confederacies, and autonomous and decentralized communities. Regional boundaries tied to racialized monikers were created during the colonial period, when the British institutionalized three entities: the Gold Coast Colony, the Asante Territory, and the Northern Territories. During colonization, the Asante and Northern Territories became protectorates, while the Gold Coast Colony was a European settlement. In the colony, British efforts focused on interventions and practices to assimilate "natives" into civil service. In the Northern Territories, chiefs were designated by colonial administrators and based on ethnicity (Darkwah and Ampofo 2008).

Anthropological monographs did much of the work on ethnic classification systems in colonial Ghana (see Manoukian [1951] 2017; Murdock 1959). Meyer Fortes, E. E. Evans-Pritchard, and Alfred Radcliffe-Brown all gained prominence in British social anthropology for their work on structural functionalism in West Africa. Ethnicities were prescribed as correspondent to language groups, regional affiliations, modes of production, and social organization.[4] Indigenous groups became tribes, with rules and cultural patterns delineated by anthropologists (Pierre 2012). The native, then, became both tribalized and racialized in contrast to European whiteness—with racialization "subsumed" under the notion of tribal affiliation (Eke 1990; Pierre 2012). For example, R. S. Rattray (1932), in *The Tribes of the Ashanti Hinterland*, divided tribes into the two broad categories "primitive" and barbaric."[5] Fortes and Evans-Pritchard published *African Political Systems* in 1940, which designated types of African political systems—the centralized state society and the acephalous, or "stateless," with collectivist governance through elders or big men. The same year, Evans-Pritchard published *The Nuer* about pastoral groups in East Africa. For sixty years, Fortes wrote about Tallensi communities of the Northern Territories with little mention of slavery and only cursory attention to colonialism's impact on social organization.

Scholarly androcentrism as well as denotations of difference that do not address race, the slave trade, and primordialism suffuses the ethnographic record (Mama 2001). Groups with centralized governments and Christian missionaries were considered more manageable (Greene 2011). Less stratified communities, with fewer hierarchies, were considered "naturally obstinate" (Holsey 2008, 97). For Konkomba-, Nanumba-, and Sisala-speaking communities, the designation of "statelessness" missed how power networks formed around resource management and access as well as variegated political alliances (Swanepoel 2009). Many northern communities were brutally depopulated by intergenerational slave raiding, first through domestic economies of enslavement, then the transatlantic slave trade. Prior to and during the transatlantic trade, gun and ammunition prohibitions instituted north of Kumasi facilitated successful slave raids for the Asante and European colonists (Brukum 2003). People from hinterlands were regular prisoners of war, and captives of Asante raids were incorporated into domestic slave economies or sold to Europeans. Some Dagaba and Tallensi communities sought environmental protection by relocating to inaccessible hills, caves, and community-made tunnels to create "remoteness" from increasingly common trade routes (Kankpeyeng 2009). Remoteness, then, was an avoidance tactic that strove to confer protection from harm, kidnap, and capture. However, that remoteness also became an index of statelessness British administrators used to codify ethnic classifications.

The colonial perspective about the Northern Territories as a free peasantry continued when the area became a British protectorate in 1901. Divestment and extraction were the protocol, with a particular lack of interest and investment in schools and hospitals (Thomas 1973). Failures in direct taxation, the most lucrative aspect of British control of the region, instigated extractive labor efforts, where men were conscripted for state-sponsored and privately funded work in railway and road construction, foresting, and mining (Wiemers 2017).

Oral histories detail how secrecy, silence, and intentional forgetfulness are common habits of slavery nonremembrance in Ghana (Apoh, Anquandah, and Amenyo-Xa 2019). There are also archival records that trace the racial politics of slavery and its link to unfree status. Trevor Getz (2004) studied how Ghanaian Supreme Court case transcripts use slave routes as a site of provenance for land cases, taking note of the way religious affiliation marked a person's susceptibility to captivity, and showed how these social stratifications engendered a person's vulnerability to enslavement. In several court cases, language and non-Christian status were shortcut denotations of enslaveability. Colonists misidentified enslaved Muslim people as Hausa, overlapping language, ethnicity, and religion, because the northern savanna was a significant place of residence for migratory groups who became enslaved (Getz 2004, 168). Captives forcibly transported through the city of Salaga were often classified as Gurunsi (also Grussie, Grunshi; Thorsen-Cavers 2006), a homogenizing ethnic category that collapses an array of ethnic groups from what is now the border between Ghana and Burkina Faso (Kuba and Lentz 2020).

Many porters I know consider towns and villages near Salaga their home. Classified by the British as part of the Northern Territories and considered part of the Northern Region until 2018, the town of Salaga is in the East Gonja District, which is now part of the Savannah Region. Remnants of Salaga's significance in the harrowing journey to captivity and enslavement are memorialized in the slave-washing wells and pits littered around the town (Kankpeyeng 2009). At the Salaga Museum, a paltry but powerful exhibition displays rusted spears and shackles unearthed in the city. Archaeological projects identified slave warehouses and barracoons at the center of town, where captives were held before their forced walking journey to coastal dungeons (Anquandah, Kankpeyeng, and Apoh 2014). As recently as 2022, a signboard tied to a baobab tree at the main bus station announced, "Welcome to Salaga Slave Market."

Ayesha Harruna Attah's (2019) novel *The Hundred Wells of Salaga* tells a gripping story of two women, Aminah and Wurche, as they navigate the turbulent uncertainty of the slave trade in precolonial nineteenth-century Ghana. From the sixteenth to the nineteenth century, Salaga was one of the most important West African cities for the commerce of gold, kola nuts, and captive Africans (M. Johnson 1986). By the eighteenth and nineteenth centuries, Salaga was home to the largest market for enslaved people, where one hundred wells were built to wash captives before their sale. Drawing on these actual events, Attah begins Aminah's story with a happy teen whose idyllic life is occasionally disrupted by caravans of stolen people passing through her town. The second principal female character, Wurche, is of noble status that is immediately known as a beneficence of slavery. Attah deftly mentions how growing stockpiles of alcohol and ammunition diminish Wurche's father's capacity to strategize against Asante, British, and German encroachment. Attah uses these storylines to show how women negotiate patriarchal norms and the way class structures agency. A town raid plunges Aminah into enslavement; the young woman initially imagines herself saved from the "big water" (Attah 2019, 66). Instead, she becomes Wurche's property. Wurche is more interested in her father's war room than a marriage alliance to shore up the safety of the community, an outcome that speaks to Attah's refusal to present a filial and homogeneous African experience.

Attah's portrayal of class, social location, and slavery is unflinching in its gendered analysis of class difference and steadfast in showing how characters come of age against the pains of oppression. This dual effort is often absent in the ethnographic record of the afterlife of slavery in Ghana.[6] With empathy for a constellation of characters and demands of readers to hold emotional space for villains and martyrs, Attah makes a sophisticated assessment of the way normative behaviors work in tandem with sites of authority to legitimate abuses of power. Bearing resemblance to the way my student Steven used regional disparity to make sense of colonialism and race, *The Hundred Wells of Salaga* breathes life into the healing power of holding space for multiple truths (McDonald 2019). The novel holds what Eswatini feminist sociologist Patriçia McFadden (2018) described as "contemporarity," which is a holistic evaluation of lived experiences and its liberatory and oppressive alignments. To make sense of the way habits and practices lay claims to autonomy, modernness, or freedom, whether individual or collective, Attah's narrative power of holding multiple truths creatively reveals Ghanaian ambivalence about regional disparities and uses social discourse to navigate the lives and afterlives of slavery and colonialism.

In a similar fashion, government initiatives that acknowledge and memorialize slavery are rife with ambivalence towards blackness and diaspora tourism. The tourism industry both highlights and obscures the history of slavery in Ghana as well as its continued significance in the state's development and investment agendas. For example, in September 2018, Ghanaian president Nana Akufo-Addo formally launched the "Year of Return, Ghana 2019" while on a visit to Washington, DC. US Congress members Sheila Jackson Lee of Texas and Gwen Moore of Wisconsin attended the event to show support (D. L. Brown 2021). Representative Jackson Lee's remarks heralded the timeliness of the Ghanaian initiative, citing that it paired well with congressional efforts to pass H.R. 40, a bill that would establish a reparations commission on US slavery and the legacies of racial inequity. Piggybacking the references to the African diaspora, President Akufo-Addo said, "We know of the extraordinary achievements and contributions they made to the lives of the Americans; it is important that this symbolic year—400 years later—we commemorate their existence and their sacrifices" (quoted in Tetteh 2019). Harking back to the arrival of African people in the United States in 1619, Akufo-Addo then called on African-descendant people to return to Africa in a "major landmark spiritual and birth-right journey" and described Ghana as the "key travel destination for African Americans and the African diaspora" (quoted in Yeboah 2019).

After Akufo-Addo's announcement, there was a boom in visas issued by the US embassy for travel to the country. In 2019, eighty thousand more tourist visas were issued to US travelers than usual (Reality Check Team 2020). The yearlong campaign brought celebrity visitors the likes of Cardi B, Naomi Campbell, Nicole Ari Parker, Rosario Dawson, and others, who shared picturesque stories on social media under the hashtag #YearOfReturn. The Year of Return also coincided with the biennial Pan-African Historical Theatre Festival (PANAFEST) in the Central Region, near the Cape Coast Castle slave dungeon and Elmina Castle. The 2019 Year of Return closed out with the cultural festival Afrochella,[7] at El Wak Stadium in Accra. The day-into-night festivities included music performances from Tiwa Savage, King Promise, and others, as well as food and fashion showcases from young talents from across the continent.

As a blend of commemoration, celebration, and commercialization, the Year of Return also drew on Ghana's long-standing efforts toward substantive political and social engagement with the diaspora. In the early 1960s, there was a bourgeoning expatriate community of African Americans that included Maya Angelou, Pauli Murray, St. Clair Drake, and Julian Mayfield. Trinidadian Pan-Africanist scholar George Padmore was special adviser to President Nkrumah and served as a major figure in the implementation of the African Affairs Bureau in Ghana. Nkrumah hosted artists, activists, and organizers including Martin Luther King Jr., Richard Wright, and Malcolm X. In 1961, Nkrumah provided Shirley Graham Du Bois and W. E. B. Du Bois a residence in the well-heeled former colonial quarter of Cantonments in Accra (see Andersson 2016; Shipley and Pierre 2007). In 1985, the Ghanaian government turned the home into the Du Bois Centre for Pan-African Culture to commemorate W. E. B. Du Bois, who is also buried at the site. In the 1990s, the Rawlings government supported renovation of the forts and castles in the Central Region that once served as slave barracoons. An embrace of historical archaeology during renovations also spurred the growth of the material collections at the National Museum (Anquandah 2018). During the fiftieth anniversary of independence in 2007, President Kufuor initiated the Joseph Project to commemorate the two hundredth anniversary of the abolition of slavery. The name of the project is in reference to the biblical Joseph, who was enslaved in Egypt but later returned to rule. These overtures to Pan-Africanism or transnational blackness, with a nod to Christianity, were a lucrative revenue stream. Estimates suggest that the Year of Return generated approximately US$1.9 billion for the Ghanaian economy (Awal 2019). The name served as a subtle encouragement to Africans in the diaspora to come to Ghana. Like the Joseph Project, the Year of Return directed tourism with a consumer approach to slavery while proffering blackness as a form of cosmopolitanism (Holsey 2013).

During his 2018 remarks, President Akufo-Addo said, "Together on both sides of the Atlantic, we'll work to make sure that never again will we allow a handful of people with superior technology to walk into Africa, seize their people and sell them into slavery. That must be our resolution, that never again, never again!" (quoted in Tetteh 2019). In addition to the oversimplification of the transatlantic slave trade being the result of "superior technology," Akufo-Addo's administration directed no funding or marketing toward slavery-related tourism sites outside of southern Ghana. For instance, in addition to being the site of a fortress wall built to protect inhabitants from the relentless attacks of slave raiders, the village of Gwollu, on the northwestern border with Burkina Faso, is also the burial site of the former president Dr. Hilla Limann (Reed 2012, 108). Most historical slave markets and slave trade routes are in the three northern regions (Northern, Upper East and Upper West) as well as the Brong-Ahafo and Volta Regions (Anquandah, Kankpeyeng, and Apoh 2014). Salaga and the former slave camps of Kassena-Nankana were never mentioned, even though a half million people from northern Ghana were enslaved between the eighteenth and nineteenth centuries (Der 1998, 29).

In June 2020, the Ministry of Tourism and Diasporic Affairs held a conference at the Du Bois Centre to renounce the killing of George Floyd and extrajudicial violence against Black people in the United States. President Akufo-Addo then requested that Floyd's name be commemorated on the walls of the Diaspora African Forum at the center (Ohene 2020). During the wreath-laying part of the ceremony, the minister of tourism, Barbara Oteng-Gyasi, implored African Americans to simply "come home" (Asiedu 2020).[8] In October 2020, the government signed a memorandum of understanding with the W. E. B. Du Bois Foundation of Harvard University to "develop, rebrand, operate and manage the Du Bois Centre" (GNA 2020). Some celebrated the announcement as an opportunity to renovate and expand the complex (Ghanaian Times 2023). Members of the African-American Association of Ghana were less than thrilled by the announcement, which revived rumors about efforts to repatriate Du Bois's remains to the United States. The Coalition to Preserve the Pan African Legacy of W. E. B. Du Bois opposed the plans, which, in addition to turning management over to Harvard, included dropping "Pan-African" from the name and renaming the center the Du Bois Museum Foundation.

In late 2020, a #BeyondTheReturn campaign launched to highlight Ghana's potential investors and "deepen the connection between Ghana and the African diaspora" (https://beyondthereturngh.com/about-us/). Around the same period, Ugandan feminist Rosebell Kagumire (2020) published an essay that rhetorically asked whether Black lives matter in Africa. Kagumire's searing essay raised alarms about the often-overlooked reality of racial injustice within Africa, suggesting that the Black Lives Matter movement, while originating in the United States, was part of reinvigorated efforts and ongoing struggle against political marginalization and police brutality in Africa. A year into the COVID-19 pandemic, which included enforced social distancing and widespread business closures, a #FixTheCountry campaign began on social media and quickly evolved into nationwide public demonstrations in Ghana. The key objectives of the campaign were demands on the government to address rising inflation and unemployment and their disproportionate impact on young people. Under the slogan "Citizens over party," activists called for improved public services, especially in education, health care, and infrastructure, as well as greater accountability and transparency about government spending. Several months following the solemn government-led commemoration of George Floyd at the Du Bois Centre, Accra organizers and activists faced their own police violence, arrest, and injury (Adamu 2020). In June 2021, the Ghana police and military fired live rounds at organizers during protests against the mob death of Kaaka (Ibrahim Mohammed), a #FixTheCountry campaign activist (S. Ansah 2021). Concurrent with their violent in-person encounters with the state, feminists, activists, and organizers used social media platforms to raise awareness about police violence and corruption and drew parallels between the struggle for decolonization in Africa and racial justice elsewhere. These connections are not new, but they have inspired new faces and voices to enter the chat.

Kagumire's and others' witness accounts and detailed observations of the horrid similarities between police repression and government unaccountability in the United States, Kenya, and Nigeria serve as a stark reminder of the multifaceted nature of spatial acts (McKittrick 2006). As Katherine McKittrick discusses, spatial acts are multifaceted processes that often hearken to physical spaces but more generatively reflect the histories and experiences of Black people, especially Black women, metaphorically, theoretically, and experientially. In that sense, then, the Year of Return and Beyond the Return memorialize and celebrate survivability and resilience. In other ways, as a spatial act, both of these campaigns and their associated activities gave attention to the labor of alternative geographies operating alongside state practices. Fix the Country gave witness to the concealed expendability attached to Black experiences in Ghana. While ensconcing blackness within the sensibilities of shared heritage in the afterlife of slavery, it is also imperative to take note of the fractal and temporal communities that struggle against precarity and marginalization. Juxtaposing the celebratory aspects of initiatives like the Year of Return with the ongoing struggles against police repression and government unaccountability develops a more nuanced understanding of the complex realities of life in Accra and elsewhere.

*   *   *

Years ago, on a Friday night in 2009, my friends and I were invited to a beach bar and open-air nightclub in the central business district of Accra. Even though just five minutes' walk from the heart of Makola Market, after sunset, the energy of the area shifts from brisk trade to festive and reposed. The bustle of the Accra Arts Centre slows and the parking lot near Kwame Nkrumah Memorial Park is empty, allowing the crashing waves of the Atlantic Ocean to be heard from Atta Mills High Street. In an alley between the memorial park and the vegan restaurant owned by African Hebrew Israelites in Ghana, our group of five, Kwate, Okaifor, Nathaniel, Panyin, and me followed a stream of people through a lane of homes to arrive at the bamboo-walled entrance of Akuma Village. It was reggae-music night, and Beres Hammond boomed through the speakers. The requisite Jamaican and Pan-African flags flapped vigorously in the ocean breeze. As we waited to enter, we greeted three Rastafarian elders as they smoked weed and chatted around a bonfire. After paying the gate fee, our friend who arrived earlier, Kwate suggested that we skip the dance floor and head to the bar first. On his suggestion, we ordered cocktails in hollowed pineapples decorated with mango and coconut skewers. The din of ocean waves competed with the reggae rhythms that floated through the air. It was a cloudless night, and the light of the moon shone on the waters and shores. Groups of partygoers sat on bamboo seats organized in semicircles around fire pits.

Kwate, Okaifor, and Nathaniel settled on bamboo chairs circling the fire while Panyin and I sat on the rock formation that rose high above the sand. We sipped fruity cocktails, spotting Jamestown Lighthouse down the shore in one direction and Christiansborg (Osu) Castle to the east. We were miles down the shore from the more pristine and tourist-filled beach scene of Labadi. The sounds of the ocean waves blended with the music playing above our heads. Together with the crackle of burning wood, it created a serene atmosphere. After a while, Kwate, who had been the person to tell the rest of us about this tucked-away beach club, stood and invited me on a walk down the shore. Also, a graduate student conducting fieldwork in Accra, Kwate learned about the reggae spot through his work with the Ga fishermen in Usshertown. Fishermen gather at daybreak to work their nets, and one early morning Kwate bumped into a group of partygoers departing Akuma Village while on his way to the beach for fieldwork. The first time he went to Akuma Village, he partied hard and also ran into some fishermen on his way out of the club. I shared my own embarrassing story about running into porters as they readied for work while I was having post-party breakfast at dawn. We laughed as we strolled, slowly, in the direction of Jamestown. The bright light of the moon lit the sand. Kwate and I were the only people on the beach until we saw a group of folks sitting around a small fire in the distance. It was difficult to make out their faces, but Kwate held up his pineapple and nodded in acknowledgment of their presence. Someone responded "Ras-Tafar-I" as we moved closer to the young women and men. We all fist-bumped and made small talk, moving through Ga and Twi before settling into a mishmash of Twi, pidgin English, and Hausa. Kwate and I introduced ourselves to Ibram and Amera, who invited us to sit with them. Amera and another woman wore ankle-length skirts, and their hair was covered. They sipped the nonalcoholic Malta Guinness, so I wondered aloud whether they were Rastas, Muslims, or neither. Amera replied, "Somehow," which is a way to acknowledge the question while also evading an answer. When the conversation moved on, she turned and asked if I was from the States. Parroting her earlier response, I answered, "Somehow." We smiled at our shared avoidance and settled into a conversation about reggae.

As we chatted, I noticed a large aluminum basin partially filled with soapy water and an empty sachet of powdered laundry detergent beside the pan. There were also clothes laid on the dry rocks with stones placed on the corners to keep them from blowing away. The pan belonged to Amera. Everyone in the group worked at the market. Ibram ran shea butter between market sellers and the traders at the arts center. In between, he worked as a *kayanu* (male porter) with his brother. Amera portered between the National Lottery office and Tema Station. Her cousin sold beads around the same area. The four had settled into an easy friendship and had been inseparable the last six months. None had steady accommodations in the city. They are all from northern Ghana, except Kwei. His family home is in Accra, but he had been primarily houseless the last two years. During our conversation, Ibram referred to Amera as his wife. She laughed but immediately corrected with "Just friends." Through most of the conversation, we learned that everyone in the group tries to look out for one another when they sleep in the open streets of the closed market. Kwei befriended a Rasta named Ital whom he met at a timber market buying discarded plywood to build a seaside lean-to. Ital told Kwei about the safety of sleeping on the beach, when you set up near the moored fishing boats. Kwei gave the rundown to his friends, and they explored the areas. Checking it out, they appreciated how the boats provided some ground cover and privacy. Most of the fishermen

were indifferent to their loitering as long as they didn't disturb their bundles
of fishing nets. Most nonresidents avoided the area because of the sandy,
damp air or a fear of Mami Wata,[9] but, given the decently maintained public toilet and washroom close by, the group decided to try out sleeping and
hanging out around the area most nights. The reggae music was a bonus for
the four friends, Ital and his friend were chill, and they all relished being
able to wash their clothes, rest, and relax on the beach, mostly unbothered.

When we met the friends, they had been staying around the beach for a
few weeks. It was the most consistent sleeping spot they had for months. The
beach was a sharp contrast to their previous sleeping spots, which oscillated
between the overturned tables of trader stalls, trash-strewn alleyways, and
the bare sidewalks. The area's night security guard shooed them away during evening rounds, which only afforded naps rather than a whole night's
sleep. Before the beach spot, those were the best places to sleep, mainly since
the night watchman only patrolled in between his own naps. Market security, in general, is often the nighttime counterpart to the daytime nemesis of
Accra Metropolitan Assembly (AMA) enforcement. Donning red vests and
armed with machetes, AMA workers march through Makola Market and de-
stroy the "unauthorized" stalls of traders who have either not paid their
taxes or not rented space through formal networks (Nyabor 2019). Their swift
removal is instrumental to the maintenance of stratified order for city governance (Biney 2014). On the few occasions that Amera and Ibram found
themselves in the way of regulators during a raid, they were unceremoniously
scuffed and scraped in the melee.

Whenever I went to Akuma Village with my research assistant friend
Esther we walked down the beach to spend time with Amera and her
friends. As time wore on, two Rastas, Irie and Ital, who had been the first
to settle the area, had enough wood planks from loading pallets to build a
sleeping shack on the shoreline.[10] Ital and Irie were in their thirties; Amera
and her friends were in their late teens and early twenties. Amera and her
friends accumulated sleeping mats and a charcoal pot that they stored
with the Rastas during their workday. They rarely used the pot because it
was cheaper to buy street food like yam and pepper or boiled eggs. Amera
did not like Irie. She referred to him as Karyarie (a portmanteau of Irie and
karya, a Hausa word for "lie"). A few weeks earlier, Irie's claim of Jamaican
origin fell apart the night they all met a group of Jamaicans on vacation.

Amera told my assistant that the lack of a lingua franca between her and Irie did not keep her from understanding his frequent invitations to sleep in the shack with him.

Most days, the multigenerational and (perhaps) multinational group agreed on someone to keep watch over their things at the beach spot. There was a general sense of indifference and kindness between the Rastas and the porters, but unconcern quickly turned to staunch solidarity when occasional confrontations about the space arose from others. The fishermen in the area let them alone, but sometimes rowdy partygoers or other market workers came around. Sometimes, strong words were exchanged, but no fistfights ensued. At the market with friends, Amera and Husena worked through most of the day together. However, Amera, Husena, Kwei, and Ibram all agreed to part ways with whoever was around at the end of the day. Each person was expected to arrive at the beach alone. Husena said there would be too many personalities if they allowed more people "to their sweet spot." Amera enjoyed Ital's occasional admonishments about consuming meat. They all rarely ate it. It was too expensive. With the ease of living most of them had not experienced in several months, the group relished their salutary solidarity about the beach space.

Accra is an epicenter of social imaginaries about modernity and expressions of necropolitical modernness. The city and the market both illuminate how distance from the dominant powers of access devalues certain bodies, where market vibrancy relies on all manner of physical labor imperiled and vulnerable. The rejection of capitalist accumulation, the exaltation of Ras Tafari (Emperor Haile Selassie I) and Marcus Garvey, and the goal of repatriation to Africa are well-known parts of the global Rastafarian movement. But the "cool culture" of Rastas smoking weed at Akuma Village while listening to reggae music did not extend to economic mobility for the two men excluded from employment access because of their beliefs and their overall unrespectability politics. Despite their explicit subordination within the market, Amera and her friends and the Rastas are not the diasporic kinships imagined in the fanfare of the Year of Return. Still, the beach dwellers have a haven within marginality that actively withdraws from harm through their efforts to create safety for themselves.

*   *   *

Inside Makola Market, there are few full-service restaurants that also offer shelter during inclement weather. Most eateries are outdoor affairs, where plastic tables and chairs are loosely organized, or lunch spots, with wooden benches angled as tables and seats in the open air. Moses felt fortunate to sell kebabs at Jubilee Restaurant. The restaurant opened in the early morning to be prepared for the high foot traffic of the business district lunch crowd. The location just past the entrance to Arch Parking was stellar for business. During the unpredictable and intermittent downpours of the rainy season, customers were not deterred from lunching at Jubilee since the outdoor dining room benefited from being breezy as well as fully covered. Moses also had a profitable agreement with the restaurant owner. As he sold kebabs, Moses also supervised the grill for *banku* and tilapia orders. Moses paid a nominal fee for the space on restaurant property and used the restaurant's storeroom. This allowed Moses to purchase charcoal and oil in bulk, which saved him time and money as he set up the huge grill drum each day. I have known Moses for the better part of a decade and have enjoyed many of his kebabs as I waited out rainstorms or for latecomers for meetings.

In June of 2015, I stopped by Rawlings Park to look for Moses. It had been three years since my last visit to Ghana, and we had lost touch. WhatsApp had gotten popular by then, but our communication had dwindled to holiday texts. It was midday Thursday, with the usual pulse of market life as I crossed Kojo Thompson Road. The cacophony of sounds, from the impatient honk of taxi and *trotro* drivers to the singsong phrases sellers use to entice customers, were unchanged, but there were differences on the square. Jubilee Restaurant was renamed, suggesting new owners, and a new sidewalk fence between the parking lot and sidewalk facilitated tidier movement across Rawlings Park.

At the threshold of the restaurant, there was still a kebab stand. Charcoal was neatly arranged in the pit. That gave me hope that Moses was nearby. A lanky teenager approached with onions and peppers in hand. After we offered greetings to one another, I asked about Moses. The young man was new on the job and did not know Moses or the owners of the new restaurant. A bit disappointed, I thanked him and walked back toward High Street. I roamed the market to look for some of the traders and porters I had come to know over the previous years.

It was a hot afternoon, and most porters on the square had sought refuge from the sun in the shade cast by the emptied morning delivery trucks. Porters who arrive at Rawlings Park early usually do the work of unloading bulk items from delivery trucks to market warehouses. The work is steady through the morning. Discarded truck tires were turned into provisional chairs. Some women flattened cardboard boxes and napped between the parked trucks that would again be loaded in the late afternoon.

It felt good to reorient myself to the space as I lapped Rawlings Park, passed Accra General Post Office, and moved along Asafoatse Nettey Road. Near Barclays Bank, I noticed some of the sellers I knew. As I approached, many of them followed the afternoon pleasantries with "Long time!" I complimented a few about their inventory changes. Eunice had upgraded from the secondhand clothes hawked on her outstretched arms to a pop-up stall. The metal card table had collapsible legs, which made it easy to dissemble if she needed to rush away from AMA patrollers. Aunty Comfort used to neatly stack red and orange peppers in heaps on a bright cloth laid on the pavement. Her tidy pyramids of assorted vegetables were now displayed on well-oiled wooden boards. And instead of being wedged between the spaces of parked cars, Comfort's stand was now nestled just past the pedestrian entrance to Rawlings Park by Market Street. After chatting for a bit, I bought a few vegetables out of courtesy and continued on my walk.

As I rounded back to the park, moving toward the taxi rank, I heard someone call my name. Turning, I saw Moses waving vigorously from just outside of the park. I had not found him; he had found me. The clues of prosperity were visible on him. Although still slim, Moses had gained a bit of weight since the last time we had seen each other. Moses was wearing a matching wax-print outfit (described as "up and down"), fashioned in a slim-cut pair of colorful trousers, the trim of the cuff perfectly coordinated with the collar of his shirt.

We shook hands and exchanged greetings. We talked about the onset of rainy season and lamented the Accra flooding that was sure to accompany the showers. In a sign of mutual affection, we continued in our handshake. Telling Moses that I looked for him over at Jubilee Restaurant, I commented that all the faces were new there. Annoyance immediately swept across his face. Moses released our handshake and placed his hands on his hips as he sucked his teeth.

"Those new people are not nice at alllll. At allllll," he said, drawing out the end of his words for emphasis.

I asked why. Instead of answering the question, Moses asked if I had time to walk with him. When we ran into each other, he was on his way to give a friend some money at the secondhand clothing market Kantamanto. Moses didn't want to keep them waiting, but he also wanted us to catch up. I hesitated. There was still time to get a shared-ride taxi that beat the onslaught of rush hour traffic. Sensing my hesitation, Moses pulled lightly on my hand and said, "Let's go. We'll get *dege* on the way." *Dege*, made from millet couscous, milk, and sugar, is a refreshing and filling cool drink with a consistency near to yogurt.[11] Persuaded by the suggestion, I started the walk with Moses to Kantamanto Market, about twenty minutes away.

Kantamanto Market, which is near to but quite distinct from Makola Market, is the largest secondhand clothing market in the city, affectionately or derisively also known as "Bend Down Boutique" (depending on social class). There are about thirty thousand traders at Kantamanto who sell clothes, footwear, household bedding, and appliance parts (Okoye 2017). It requires patience and practice to move through the sections of the market, as vendors have items for sale hanging from tent poles or spread out on massive tarps on the ground. Clothes are sometimes piled five feet high, and vendors sometimes place the left and right shoe in separate heaps to deter thieves from making quick grabs.

After we briskly walked through several lanes, we met up with Moses's friend at his sale spot, which included a massive pile of sneakers and smaller stack of soccer jerseys. Before they step behind a divider, which is made of flattened storage bundles and stitched together as a quick dressing room, Moses's friend invites me to browse. The divider is composed of the polyester that is commonly used to ship secondhand clothes to Ghana from Australia, the United States, and China. Meanwhile, in the few minutes I waited, three vendors solicited me with either "America nii?" or "What are you looking for? Let me help you," as they walked by holding up batteries, dish towels, and shoes. A few minutes after that, the most enterprising of the three returned, carrying a pair of sandals and sneakers that on first look appeared to be my size. The vendor sat in front of me on a stool that had been nestled under his arm to encourage me to try them on. Just as I was shaking my head no, Moses stepped out of the dressing room. Cutting a quick glance his way, the vendor was making a silent request for Moses to allow him to finish his pitch. I smiled and said, "Next time, next time." Turning to Moses, I asked, "What happened to my *dege*?" Laughing, Moses said, "I didn't forget. This way." As he turned down one lane and then another that led out of the indoor sale areas of Kantamanto, I followed Moses back toward Mamleshie Road. Once we reached the bright yellow-and-red signs of the latex and foam mattress depot, we stopped in front of a wheelbarrow and crate turned into a drink stand, where one woman was dipping into a huge calabash and pouring chilled *dege* into plastic cups. A second, younger woman, perhaps an apprentice, washed used cups in one bowl of soapy water with a clear rinsing bowl beside it. The mound of dirty cups suggested that business had been brisk for the day, and inside the calabash, the typically huge ice blocks were melted to cubes. These were all signs of good *dege*, where the millet couscous was perfectly shaped in a boba-type fashion and a sweet accompaniment to the sweetened milk. After making our purchases, Moses suggested that we settle on a nearby bench.

Moses was in a confiding mood. He updated me on what he had been up to since last we saw each other. It had been nearly two years since he left work at Jubilee Restaurant. He was now working with a friend, securing steel drums to be used as barbeque pits and selling charcoal wholesale. Most lucratively, he managed the distribution of wholesale goods that arrived from overseas. As the person who now connected people from all over Makola Market, Moses held more status than in years past. But it was not without struggle at Jubilee and a bumpy transition. Moses was fired when the owner suspected someone of pilfering frozen food and other restaurant items from the storeroom. The manager, whom Moses suspected as the culprit, in turn accused Moses of the crimes. One morning, as Moses reported to work, the manager and owner both sat at a table. The owner waved him over and, as he approached, said, "Good morning, Musa. Come." Moses said he felt his body stiffen as he approached the table. I asked, "Musa?"

"Yeah, so when I first came to Accra and told people my name was Musa, they would say, 'You don't look like a northerner,' because they think all of us have ceremonial marks, and I don't have any. Plus, I'm a bit fat," he said, pinching the tiny fold of skin at his waist. "After hearing that so many times, I started calling myself Moses. It's just easier."

In that moment, I didn't ask Moses to explain what he meant, because I had heard people say "northern looking" countless times and had a good idea of what he meant. Not wanting to disrupt the flow of the conversation, I didn't follow up then, but "northern looking" indexes some commonly held assumptions and stereotypes about the millions of ethnically diverse people who come from northern regions.

Continuing the story, Moses said he stood at the table "as if I was a child, waiting to be scolded," while the manager and owner closely studied his face. Asserting his superordinate position, the owner did not invite Moses to sit down, and the manager looked on smugly. Moses sensed the manager had made a case against him in his absence. His suspicions were confirmed when the owner told Moses he was "sacking him" and that there was "evidence." Bemused, Moses asked what it was. The owner said Moses had access to the storeroom. Moses was the first person who arrived at the restaurant in the morning, which gave him ample opportunity to take things. Moses thought both of those reasons were more a testament to his trustworthiness, but he did not voice his dispute. Finally, the last bit of "proof" the owner offered was that Moses had lied about his name. The manager then chimed in that Moses's being from the north explained why Moses was "lax on the cleaners" (who were also northerners) and paid the delivery porters (also northerners) "too much," although "too much" was Moses's insistence on paying fair wages to the women who loaded for the business. With the "evidence laid out," Moses said the owner dismissed him from the table. Moses was disappointed but unsurprised by the turn of events and sure the outcome could not be changed. Disagreement about what belonged to whom ensued when Moses tried to collect his meat items from the freezer. The manager rushed one of the servers back to work when the server tried to help Moses pack up his charcoal. The final insult was when the owner told him to wait until the regular end-of-the-month payday to receive his wages.

"It wasn't because of the lie," said Moses. "That was just an excuse."

Moses intimately understood discrimination as antiblackness even if he didn't name it. Throughout the story, he lamented how being a *northerner* was the rationale for his termination. Thankfully, it took only a few days for Moses's neighbor to help him identify another space to sell kebabs. A few months later, Jubilee closed for renovations. After being shuttered for six months, including the lucrative Easter season, Jubilee was sold to a new owner. Moses felt vindicated by the restaurant's closure, which coincided with his new, more lucrative job in import-export. Still, he spurned his neighbor's optimism that getting fired from Jubilee was what helped him garner more lucrative employment.

As we finished our *dege*, we shifted to more upbeat banter and funny updates about our family and friends. Our conversation wound down, and we started our walk back to the main street. As we had done in past years, Moses waited with me for my *trotro* to Apapa Junction to arrive before beginning his ride in the opposite direction toward Mamprobi. Standing at the bus stop, I jokingly asked, "So how do I call you now? Moses or Musa?"

Chuckling, he replied, "Musa is Moses. Moses is Musa. Either one. I'm around."

In conversation with the archival narratives about the north and modernness I discussed earlier, Moses's experience is not unusual. His choice to be called Moses in response to *not looking northern* may suggest many things, but the comments influenced Musa's choice to use a "less Muslim" and "less northern" name to shore up some distance from his disadvantageous position. The manager's accusation about a filial northern(er) identity dogwhistled untrustworthiness, poor judgment, and provincialism. And a lie about one's name is a tepid excuse, given how common it is for Ghanaians to have a variety of names and nicknames for different social contexts. First, there are "outdooring" celebrations across Ghana, many of which involve a naming ceremony, libation, and prayers of affirmation, safety, and prosperity for a child. Also widely used are "English" baptismal and Quranic names in educational settings. Then there are given names that correspond with the day someone is born. Close family members regularly use these as your in-the-house name.

Then there are the social clues as to why Moses was read as less northern. In Ghana, bigger bodies have historically been often associated with wealth, but the globalization of Western beauty trends heavily influences recent changes in the way women's bodies are perceived. Slenderness has become more desirable and stylish. For men, bigger bodies are still strongly linked to affluence, and Musa has a small, round belly on his otherwise slim frame.

This "fatness," then is symbolic of abundance but incongruent with public expectations about who is perceived as having affluence and status.

When Moses and I discussed facial marks in a later conversation, he shared how he received spiritually protective marks on his wrists and hips as part of a coming-of-age ceremony. Although facial scars were popular in his hometown, Moses did not have marks on his cheeks. The absence of facial marks was considered "less northern" despite the popularity of body modification as beauty ritual or protective spiritual practice in various ethnic groups in southern Ghana as well. During early independence, nudity, facial marking, female circumcision, and debt bondage came be to be viewed as "undesirable practices," strongly associated with people from the north and considered "inconsistent with modern times" (Cammaert 2016, 165). Although nudity, markings, and debt bondage were common across Ghana, the spotlight shone brightest on northern Ghana because of the overlapping prevalence of these various practices and growing international attention coming from the missionaries and aid agencies at work in the region. The need for a peasant class and agrarian economy to support industrialization projects meant that physical bodies symbolized capital accumulation and mobility as well as broader power struggles about land, labor, and resources. The discursive shortcut made by remarks about looking or not looking "northern" becomes part of the "afterlives of colonial urban racism" that support racialized scripts about region and desires about what it means to be modern (Ochonu 2019a, 17).

Northerner, as a term, has far more prevalence than any other regional moniker as an identity placeholder. People who reside outside of directionally northern parts of Ghana are usually characterized by ethnicity rather than region. However, this is not to suggest that ethnicity has no value in social discourse or that it matters less than race. In fact, there are a fair share of ethnic stereotypes in Ghana. Akin to the way zodiac signs are used to anticipate behaviors and attitudes, ethnicity is used to assess business acumen, personality characteristics, and romantic compatibility.

"Fanti people love school too much"; "Asante men love to argue"; "Ewe people love juju more than Christ"; "Ga people are rowdy"—all are common stereotypes about specific ethnic groups that come up in everyday conversations about ethnicity. However, in contrast, whether Konkomba, Gonja, Kotokoli, Gurunsi, Mossi, or any of the other dozens of ethnolinguistic groups of Ghana's northern regions, in southern cities like Cape Coast, Accra, Tema, and Koforidua, these diverse groups are referred to as simply "northerners" (Lentz 2006). The reverse does not ring true about "southerners" in my interviews and conversations in the Eastern and Volta Regions or in cities like Ho, Hohoe, Wa, or Tamale.

These and other observations are why I suggest that some Ghanaians use *northerner* as a discursive framework that bears more similarity to racialization than ethnicization and argue that *northerner*, as a categorization of blackness, is a racial project among Ghanaians. In the same way that slavery is a commoditized placeholder for the aspirations of diasporic tourism, the north and northerners are situated as irreconcilable impediments to neoliberalist development aims. Women head porters, in their work as rural-to-urban laborers, are surplus bodies, irrespective of their citizenship in the nation-state. Their anti-modern bodies represent a failure of access to capital accumulation and excess because their northernness is a primordial blackness hinged to slavery and an undesirability of agriculturalism. The market exchanges that porters sustain through head-loading are essential, yet antithetical to modern consumption desires. The result is antiblackness exacted on Black bodies in Black spaces and a social displacement that becomes a necessary hypervisible disposability. The palpable derision toward the north and northerners is a spatial and racial valuation located in sense-work and sentiment and suffused with material consequences. Moses and Amera are exploitable bodies because their presence in the city hinges on the essentialized unbelonging of northerners, a placeholder that collapses the class, religious, spatial, and lingustic diversity of places into a singular coded category. The north, northerners, and northernness are a crucible for naming difference, and antiblackness is the normative result.

In my effort to be sensitive to the way porters and other migrants persist within these fraught spaces, blackness and antiblackness—as affective, descriptive, and imaginative experiences—operate within an array of affinities and consequences. I use the suffix -*ness*, sometimes described as the intersubjective, to also make room for the sentient space between a state of being, selfhood, and the world around you. To be sure, antiblackness enacted by the state is a violent and deathly force in the most expansive and damaging ways. But antiblackness also lives in the shade of discourse and gesture, which also has a part to play in the social orders that relegate porters and other bodily laborers to the bottom. Still, Amera's and Musa's praxis in world making, as well as the forced flexibilities they use to wrestle against, help explain how social negotiations around blackness can index individuated, shared, pre-personal, and macrosocial contexts. Ethnography identifies how racial projects rationalize marginalization and also illuminate how people move against these violences of reducibility. By connecting historical context and recent events to the stories shared about work and shelter, I show how race and blackness are ensconced in daily life. Although racial vernaculars about "the north" reflect the deep social anxieties about modernness in Ghana, these encounters also take account of the practical sense-work people engage in to live through housing precarity and underemployment.

CHAPTER 3

Radical Listening and Haptic Sifting

This chapter uses photovoice as ethnographic method and praxis to explain how photographs, as material objects, make living archives of affirmation and community making between porters. Photovoice is a community-based action where participants use film or digital cameras to take photos of their choice. Participants then share stories about the images or the experiences and memories that the images give rise to. Photovoice is commended for its capacity to amplify community members' voices and create opportunities for participants to know and see themselves in novel ways (Shah 2015). However, a photograph's meanings can chart methodological tensions riskier than words. Thus, despite its laudable outcomes, photovoice is ensnared in discursive loops about images' representational and evidentiary value (Shankar 2016). If a picture is worth a thousand words, it can also cast a thousand tales, and stoke fears about the digital age that make it even more difficult to trust what story a photograph aims to tell. So, instead of laying bare the photographs that women took or tracing the discursive sensibilities detailed in specific images, this chapter explores the kinds of knowledges photovoice uncovered, explains photovoice as a feminist methodology, and examines how creative methods lend credibility to reciprocal fieldwork relationships and why these approaches matter in an African context.

Black feminist anthropologist Faye V. Harrison has clarified that, while there are "no feminist methods per se," there are feminist "methodologies that articulate conceptual, theoretical, and ethical perspectives on the whats, whys, and hows of research and the production of knowledge" (2007, 25). This chapter opens with a series of chance encounters at Makola Market to show

how standard anthropological methods, such as participant observation and interviews, joined with photovoice became feminist methodologies of mutuality, flexibility, and care. Photovoice complemented interviews, supplemented observations, and animated the stagnant lulls of underemployment. The interiority of waiting and boredom along with the corporeality of muscle aches, joint pains, and body soreness is difficult to discern and make legible, but photovoice crafted visual archives of daily life that reflexively critiqued ordinary days between brisk, hurried work and the tedium of head-loading.

With these precepts, this chapter takes up photovoice[1] as a feminist framework that manifests the affective contours of African diasporic relations. Initiated through photography as a fomenter of friendship, I explore picture taking as a sensory theoretic between Black women to name and explain intangible intimacies and ephemeral angsts. In the following sections, I also use leisurely activities, such as storytelling and rest, alongside cooking and hair care, as hermeneutics that engage African women separate from archetypical maternal roles. I show how women as cocreators and experts in their own lives refute the wholesale victim tropes attached to African womanhood and bring critical reflection and image creation together and away from reductive narratives about community through struggle.

Porters labor within miasmic precarity, through an embodied existentialism that need not be made into a pornography of poverty. As a method, photovoice accesses affective sensibilities, shifts attention away from photographs as evidentiary, and cues sentiment and emotion. It also holds space for care as conviviality and the boundaries of emotion, where intimacies are balms against pathologies of inequity. Storytelling, with or alongside images, explains how people develop and struggle to maintain fortitude (Bunster B. 1977). Just as a picture is a material object that circulates with a social life, the praxis of picture taking can detail bodily evocations to explain how Ghanaian girls and women sense the market, themselves, and each other.

*   *   *

Between November and January of any year, frequent trips to Makola Market are commonplace. New gadgets, seasonal imported foods, and fresh wax-print cloth entice holiday shoppers to endure traffic congestion to grab the latest goods. Boarding school and university students and Ghanaians from abroad come to shop and socialize in the capital for the Christmas season. Years ago, I took near-daily trips to Makola Market to accompany a friend who needed design supplies for her fashion business. Time was tight because Ghanaians from abroad used their Accra visits to commission spring and summer wardrobes to take along when they departed after New Year's Day. During the Christmas season of 2005, I was at the market with my friend Sheena to search for Burano lace. In our search, we struggled to move quickly against the throng of shoppers also attempting to hurry through the lanes of wax print. Imported from Italy, the fabric sold out fast. We persisted because Sheena's client was adamant about adding Burano lace panels to the sleeves of her summer suits. Two two-storied buildings occupying a street behind the Makola Market entrance sign had shops specializing in foreign fabrics. The second-to-last shop on the back end of the second building stocked what we sought. When the shop owner waved us inside, the air blowing from her fan offered little relief from the Harmattan dust that clung to our brows or the sweat rolling down our backs. Asking about the assortment of Burano lace, Sheena sank into a metal chair at the back of the shop and waited for the shop assistant to present the offerings. Already loaded with bags of thread, boning, lining, and several finished outfits, Sheena still had to make deliveries to clients in the Cantonments neighborhood. When offered sachets of ice-cold water from a cooler near the fan, we happily accepted them.

To make the most efficient use of time, I doubled back to a shop we had passed to buy rice. The large kilo bags were much cheaper than at my neighborhood market. Sheena would flash when she was finished shopping so we could head out. To "flash" is when someone uses their cell phone to contact another person, allows the call to ring once or twice, and then hangs up. This signal would let me know Sheena was finished shopping without depleting the talk-time credits on her phone. In the time between when she flashed and we met back on the street of the mall, on impulse and good deals, I bought five kilos of rice, nearly a gallon of palm oil, and a few handfuls of *alasa* and *yoyi*.[2] I had far more than I could reasonably carry and struggled to adjust my bags every twenty paces. When I reached Sheena, she was also loaded with packages, including six yards of the intricate and expensive lace that brought us to the market. Walking toward the taxi stand, we ran into Sister Akosua, a woman from my neighborhood who sells an assortment of goods at the market. Taking note of our heavy loads, Akosua rushed toward us, whistled, and called out "kayayoo" in the direction of a group of women porters sitting atop their pans on the roadside. Although my fieldwork put me in the company of porters most days, my shopping trips were usually small, so I rarely relied on their services. Rahida responded to Akosua's call, approaching with a silver-colored pan. I would come to know Rahida well in subsequent years, but that day in December was our first encounter. When Rahida reached us, she placed the basin on the ground. Akosua relieved us of our purchases and put them in the large metal bowl. When it was Sheena's turn to load, she declined, "I don't want the palm oil to stain the cloth."

Sheena's time was crunched. She needed to close out her errands to hurry back and finish her holiday orders. We thanked Akosua for her help and resumed walking toward the Tema Station taxi stand. While we waited for a gap between cars to cross High Street, Sheena received a phone call. The conversation was short, but Sheena was exasperated. The person she was going to meet was elsewhere in town. Sheena now had to travel to the Teshie-Nungua neighborhood to collect her final payment. With our plans to share a taxi disrupted, Sheena hailed her cab at Ministries, the popular name for the road where several civil services and Supreme Court buildings are located. After quick goodbyes, she hopped in the cab, and I continued to walk toward Tema Station, with Rahida silently following.

One of the oldest lorry stations in Accra, Tema Station is one of three bus terminals within easy walking distance from Makola. *Trotros*, shared rides, and dropping are all available for destinations around the city,[3] in addition to vehicles for eastward travel toward the port city of Tema. Though close to Makola, the station has its own market, where traders sell goods under bright umbrellas and hawkers stroll between cars and buses with their arms outstretched as they shout pronouncements about their wares. Gutters packed with plastic bags line the space between the sidewalk and street, and dozens of *kayayei* rest, work, and reside in the partitioning spaces where grass has long stopped growing. At the shared-ride taxi rank, cars idle to await passengers. Shared-ride taxis operate on a set route, and passengers pay a flat rate. My destination was Osu Residential, so I headed toward the four taxis lined behind the sign for "37," shorthand for 37 Military Hospital.

With trading brisk as always, I was surprised to see so many idling shared-ride taxis. As I approached the first car, the driver waved me off, pointing to the broken trunk latch with a plastic bag knotted above the license plate and looping through the missing keyhole of the trunk. My purchases would not be secure once the car filled with riders. Moving to the next available taxi, with Rahida still close behind, I realized I was at a loss about the next steps in our transaction. Rahida stood at the trunk and leaned downward. By the time the cabbie and I unloaded the items from the pan, the first taxi had filled and set off. The two remaining seats in the cab meant we would be on our way shortly. Everything was now loaded in the trunk except the rice; I turned to Rahida, asking, "How much?" In what I later learned was customary practice between porters and their customers, Rahida lowered her gaze and cupped her hands. She looked like someone with a professional commitment to the flawless presentation of modesty, but the flurry of activity instilled a sense of hurry. I handed Rahida three cedis. The corners of her mouth turned upward into a slight smile.

It was still a year before full-time fieldwork began in earnest, but with the taxi idling and Rahida and I still standing close, I wanted to make a connection related to a photography project I imagined as part of my research. After we positioned the sack of rice on the taxi floor to mark my seat, I reached for my 35 mm camera and asked Rahida if I could take her picture. Rahida's gaze shifted from the camera to the distance, then she shoved the coins into the folds of her skirt, shook her head in a barely perceptible denial, and walked off.

My impulsive misstep ended the conversation. I wondered if we misread each other's body gestures or misunderstood language. I didn't know whether Rahida's no was about the photograph. Did she think my three cedis were some sort of expectant prepayment for a portrait? With these questions swirling in my mind with no definitive answers, I sulked as the taxi crept into the slow crawl out of Tema Station. I berated myself for not explaining to Rahida why I wanted to take her photo. Truthfully, I didn't know the entire reason.

Sensing Ethnographic Diffidence

I was formally introduced to Rahida while at Makola Market the following week. During this market visit, I was playing with my camera and snapping photos of Melcom, a new supermarket on Pagan Road. The giant retailer sold an array of market goods with a Walmart-like business model where the corporation purchased at discounted bulk prices and undersold items just cheaper than the rates of most traders. Business boomed from the opening day onward. Next to the entrance, a man in a full Santa costume, including patent leather boots in ninety-degree weather, sang, "Ho—ho—ho, Merry Christmas." American Christmas carols blasted from a boombox currently on sale inside the store. The final touch in the scene was a turbine-sized fan (also for sale at Melcom) positioned over a box of shredded white paper blowing white confetti over Santa's shoulders and littering the street. I snapped a few shots of the cosplay advertising, then settled across the road for lunch. As I ate fried gizzard, green pepper, and yam on a bench next to the stall, Rahida approached, gave a slight curtsy, and introduced herself. Slight-bodied, with bright brown eyes and espresso-colored skin, Rahida appeared to be in her early twenties. She pointed to the camera slung on my shoulder and said, "I am ready." Gone were the worn-down *chale wote* and faded T-shirt dress from when she carried my groceries.[4] Rahida wore leather sandals, a satin under scarf for her hijab, and a brightly colored, striped top. The second piece of fabric, wrapped over her skirt, indicated she was married. It was Friday, so Rahida spent time with friends after Jumu'ah, the Muslim congregational prayer. When the group spotted me, Rahida decided to ask for a portrait. She wanted to send a picture to her family back home. She spoke Likpakpaln and Dagbanli fluently. English, not so much, so one of her friends translated her request from Likpakpaln to pidgin English. Surprised and happily obliged by this newly found permission, I snapped photographs of Rahida and her friends. After shooting a roll of film, we agreed to meet the following week so that I could give back the prints.

The next week I returned with the photographs from the lab, accompanied by Solomon, who worked as my research assistant and translator. We lingered around the yam stand for about thirty minutes before Rahida arrived. She was alone and said her friends couldn't make it. After introductions and greetings, I handed Rahida the stack of pictures. As she flipped through the images, Rahida's shy smile grew wide. After peering at a dozen photographs, she started to lean forward more closely, as if trying to look more deeply into the print, the bench she sat on tipped forward onto two legs. Carefully and gently touching the edges of her face in the picture, Rahida spoke with Solomon in Dagbanli, repeatedly describing herself as satisfied. Rahida explained how the outcome of our encounter was surprisingly fortuitous, given how she had only approached me to take her photograph as the result of a dare from her friends. They didn't believe Rahida and I knew each other, because she didn't speak much English and I was neither Ghanaian nor Muslim. Seeing me taking photos of Santa confirmed our taxi-stand encounter, and Rahida did want to have her picture taken that Friday because she looked nice. The only other photographs she had of herself were a couple of passport-sized pictures from a primary school enrollment form from years ago. Rahida planned to send this new photo back home. A photograph crafted a more reassuring narrative than a handwritten letter. Like most of her relatives, Rahida attended school intermittently and did not read or write Likpakpaln (her first language), Dagbanli (the lingua franca of her home region), or English (the language of instruction after second grade). Her original plan was to hire a scribe outside the Accra General Post Office and dictate a letter. This dictated letter would then be carried home by a cousin. When the correspondence was delivered, a reader would be called to share her news. Her entire household would listen to its sharing. Rahida suspected that lengthy gestural pauses and long verbal hesitancies during the read-aloud were the reader's effort to downplay the expressed hardships in the letter and embellish good news. Rahida said that the person always "wants your people to see themselves well" and ends up interpreting as they read. Furthermore, the translation and exchange in a letter depreciated the currency of the story because "the storyteller never wants to disappoint" the audience.

Situating Rahida's high hopes for her photograph's haptic and affective resonance is her effort to push against any conscripts of behavior and reject someone else's capacity to set the terms of understanding around how she fares in Accra. In embracing this analysis, this ethnographic moment strives to reconfigure the epistemologies of our exchange. In his critique of anthropology, Michel-Rolph Trouillot contends that fieldwork and its output, ethnography, regularly conflate the field as an object of study and locales "defined primarily by what happens there" rather than as locations that are always situated and intersected by an array of political, economic, and social connections. Trouillot soberly observed that, "Anthropologists never give the people they study the right to be knowledgeable or more precisely, not to have the same kind of knowledge about their societies as ethnographers" (2003, 129).

But the self-described "belly of the family," with relatives who relied on her remittances to feed the household, Rahida needed the portrait to substantiate her well-being claims and mask her occasional need to skip meals to send money home. Rahida wanted the picture to convey a modicum of success, even though a photograph, much like the letter's reader, glossed her chronic challenges. Back home, the household faced perennial food insecurities, and Rahida didn't fare much better on her own in Accra.

Rahida's reflections align with scholarly warnings against deputizing the state as the primary site to think through the contours of sociopolitical negotiation. For instance, when a recently returned family friend reported to her parents that Rahida was "far too slim," Rahida wanted the evidentiary aspects of a picture to calm their anxieties about her safety. At the same time, Rahida's request for the market backdrop in the photo reminds everyone why she is away from home in the first place. She "felt okay most days" but didn't want anyone to think she was doing "too well" because then expectations might rise about the amount of her remittances. This keen awareness about her family's worries about her health recognizes the grueling physicality of porterage, but, still, Rahida used a photograph as a means to control the stories being told about her time in Accra.

In the snapshot, the bright stripes on her shirt were not faded due to a limited range of clean attire. She recently bought the top at the Kantamanto secondhand market, so her family would read the shirt as brand new. No one in her household had more than a week's worth of clothes, so her fresh attire might confer an inventive defense against the anxiety in her mother's voice when they spoke over the phone.

As I listened to Solomon translate Rahida's words, with her reflections and picture storytelling so smooth and insightful, I decided to pitch photovoice again. After a pause between Rahida and Solomon, I said, "So I have this project I'm doing with porters about photographs . . ." while looking expectantly at Solomon. As I listened to Solomon translate, Rahida's body shifted away from the close touch of our knee-to-knee-facing position. This unmistakable signal was Rahida breaking the social intimacy of our seated position. I knew my request was failing when Rahida's back straightened. She leaned away from our cozy face-to-face posture on the bench. Solomon looked from me to Rahida as her movement spoke refusal even though no words were said aloud. Then, stretching her hand toward me, Rahida tried to push the photographs back into my hand. This rebuff was reorienting the tenor of our conversation. The shift in vibe was not lost on Solomon, who quietly piped in, "Don't worry. Next time, next time"—a regularly used refrain to soften denial or rejection in a conversation. Ignoring her outthrust hand, I handed Rahida the storage envelope from the photography studio and said, "It's cool, just share the photos with your friends who couldn't come." The mention of her friends recovered some of the conversational sour, and Rahida accepted the envelope. "When will we meet again?" I asked, looking expectantly as Solomon translated.

Rahida looked away from Solomon and vaguely replied, "Soon," tucking the envelope of photos under her arm. The shift in Rahida's stance deflated my hope that we had just concluded on a high note.

The following year "soon" took shape in the form of seeing Rahida nearly every day I spent at Makola Market. Her presence was instrumental and instructive, and I anticipated seeing her each day; she shaped so many aspects of the time I spent with porters in Accra. Rahida was new to the city the year we met, but portering at Kejetia Central Market, the largest market in West Africa in the midland city of Kumasi, eased her transition to Accra. Makola is smaller than Kejetia, but with the exhaustive improvisation, negotiating, and networking exacted on porters to make money, Rahida seemed to manage better than most. She had an ear for languages and had recently learned pidgin English from a boyfriend. Rahida had a reputation as a good fighter, having prevailed in a physical altercation by throwing pepper spice into her opponent's face.

A common strategy porters use is to appoint a leader within the friend group to settle disputes and organize on behalf of the group (Imam and Tamimu 2015). Rahida took on that role among a group of porters who embraced the lack of accommodations and lived and worked around Rawlings Park. Rahida is a witty and popular polyglot who cajoled customers into adding money when they offered small amounts of money for loads. She established relationships with a few shopkeepers for her and her friends to be the preferred loaders for their customers. Delivery drivers knew her by name and called on her to gather a requisite number of porters to unload the big trucks after their early morning arrival at the market. In addition to being a connector between porters, traders, and other laborers, Rahida facilitated dozens of introductions on my behalf between these groups, regularly offering quick quips and an unrestrained laugh at her own comedic commentary and confidence. Once, I spotted Rahida as she carried a large cardboard box of tinned milk in her robin's-egg-blue-speckled pan. The cans of milk overflowed from the top of the box. As she moved down the sidewalk from the opposite direction, with the load balanced on her head, we made eye contact through the crowd of pedestrians. I smiled in recognition as the space between us shortened. Then, Rahida suddenly lost her balance, veering a hard left toward the edge of the pavement. She was dangerously close to the street, as cars hurriedly whizzed toward the traffic circle. I was more than half a block away but rushed toward her. A second later, a comedic rhythm came to her tumbling strut as she balanced her stride, treating the curb like a gymnast would a balance beam. The cadence of her walk signaled a choreographed fake fall. Catching on, I imitated her heel to toe, one foot in front of the other, swaying as we moved toward one another. Rahida nodded that I had caught on, laughed, and then turned into an alley to continue her work.

Head-loading is arduous, fast-paced work, but Rahida's acuity and humor are quicker still. Rahida ended conversations when our high-energy banter hinted toward an ethos of interviewer-interviewee (Simpson 2007). Rahida refused photovoice and any effort to be part of any formalized aspects of fieldwork. Still, her contradictory conviviality profoundly aligns with the spirit of "politics, praxis, and poetics" of Black feminist ethnographic methodologies (McClaurin 2001; Tynes 2020). If I was at Makola having lunch with someone on Rawlings Square, Rahida would wander past the restaurant and offer a barely perceptible head nod. On other occasions, she interrupted conversations in the slender shade of beleaguered palm trees to share humorous outtakes about a recent load she carried or offer a supplement to the ensuing dialogue.

Rahida's retooling of our relationship is a place of beginnings rather than an end of ethnographic inquiry, a reimagining of "discursive, material and moral territory" with imaginative temporality (Reese 2019). Whether doing my shopping or socializing with friends near Makola, I became accustomed to Rahida's unexpected and comedic disruptions. Rahida rebuked the social dictates of our status differences and regularly interjected in conversations already slowed by the weight of translation. The ethnographic richness of Rahida's interruptions shows how refusal functions and takes shape as an innovative method for everyday life. In her participant observation, Rahida surveilled *me*, listening to my habits, never the other way around.

The somatic value in the nonlinear parts of a photographic praxis plays with the contradiction of identity and place making that occur in body, work, and place and attunes "our senses to the other affective frequencies through which photographs register" (Campt 2017, 9). Rahida's exacting disengagement with photovoice but ongoing participation and commentary about pictures brings forward how storytelling vis-à-vis images can sway against the extractive tenors of fieldwork. Rahida shows up how she wants, when she wants, and to the levels that suit her pleasures and interests. Her ways of showing up resonate with fugitive epistemologies, where experience and self are data, and lived experiences become fundamental valuations of feminist praxis (Berry et al. 2017). The circuitous nature of Rahida's declinations is Rahida's mode of making known that I am expected to do something on her behalf (Christian 1988, 68). Rahida's preemptive denials of the added labor of photovoice are a refusal "beyond the mitigation of consequences," harm reduction, or wage negotiations (Reese 2019). Rahida wanted a photograph as an archive of well-being rather than as data for a research project about porters. Rahida's dis/trust or care/less attitudes are hermeneutics of interiority fundamental to survival for Black girls and women (Cox 2015, Shange 2019). Distance and dis/trust are the encumbrance of a diss and trust. Rahida trusts me to do something for her (take pictures of her to send home) and disses participation in my research project in order to test our relationship's limits. Rahida's seemingly care/less attitude encompasses the subtle and cautionary notes of care and careless, which should never be confused with carelessness, even when her gestures signal toward that.

*   *   *

Emotions are not standard in anthropological accounts of the lives of African people, especially women. The feelings of African women are often left to literary scholars. This chapter moves against the parenthetical way feelings reside in ethnography about African women and girls. Rather than following the conventional structure of a proverbial "methods chapter" of a book, this story about Rahida is a sentient moment that takes African feminisms and photovoice as Black feminist sensory praxis. The attention to the sensory registers of affective awareness, silence, and refusal is my effort to bring method and theory together.

The horrific legacy of the objectification and thingifcation of Black women's bodies leads many narratives of African womanhood to cover the body in respectability politics or resistance (Bennett and Pereira 2013). But feminist scholars have done tremendous work on the affective sociality of emotion without a "predetermined *effect*" of histories, logics, and experiences (Stewart 2017, 193). The scholarship of African and African-descendant feminists frequently assembles how emotions sift and negotiate cisheteropatriarchy, racism, and marginalization through bodily, sensory, and aesthetic maneuvers in everyday life. In ethnography anchored in rational as well as irrational logics, ordinary tendencies, and reverberant improvisations (see Ahmed 2010; Cerwonka and Malkki 2008; Stewart 2007; Berland 2011), feminist scholars of Africa and the diaspora have long interrogated Black women's lives between and beyond the confines of body and flesh to deepen the racial literacy of affect theory (Spillers 1987; Sharpe 2014; Anumo and Onyango 2020). In *Decolonization and Afro-Feminism*, Sylvia Tamale (2020) argues that feeling, intimacy, and emotion are instructive armaments against precarity and patriarchy. Guided by this premise, I ground ethnography with feeling and emotion in order to attend to the kaleidoscopic interiorities of African women's experiences. Despite the landscapes of high surveillance Black women face (McFadden 2003), a vibrant discourse exists on the corporealities of African womanhood through visual methods (Matebeni 2013). I hope my use of photo-making, or, in Rahida's case, nonmaking, is viewed as an intimacy-building vulnerability understood as an output of care[5] and a theoretic of well-being.

Creative methods lend themselves to collective acts of resistance (Campt 2019). Using a visual praxis, with an attentiveness to the somatic, is an effort to move between pessimism and futurity as well as individual acts and community making. To be clear, photovoice as praxis cannot mend the pornography of pain baked into the way Black people's bodies are described and imaged. Nor can the disposability attached to porters' lives be fully refuted through stories that showcase women as more than a collection of tragedies and traumas, because photographs are deeply fraught in their representations of Black people. However, aligned with the way scholars across the humanities and social sciences have shown how Black women are phenomenologically situated[6] and somatically oriented[7] to photography's oppressive and liberatory power, in anthropology, the violence of ethnographic photography showcases African women as the dichotomous Other to whiteness, woman-hood, and modernity. Although there are warranted criticisms of the power of visual archives to reinforce coloniality in relation to access, subjectivity, and the circulation of images, there are also tremendous assessments of the grandeur, play, and reclamation of African femininity and selfhood articulated through photography (McKinley 2021). The recent use of visual methods to engage the lived experiences of African women, specifically young women and girls, have interrogated the poverty porn associated with humanitarian intervention (de Laat and Gorin 2016), the ways that photography uses cosmopolitan tropes as African-modernity projects (McKinley 2021), and how unclothing and nudity become a political antithesis of modernity (Cammaert 2016). I conceive of a visual praxis as a relational rubric that theorizes the *hows* of everyday life as deeply personal and embodied iterations of political and material contexts people strive to negotiate in their own distinct ways. For most porters, the concern is not about what photographs capture, freeze, or memorialize but how images situate the contours of relationships, how they are organized and evaluated. Images are an affective mechanism for noting emotional and social proximities that are not otherwise apparent.

Since 2007, I have conducted fieldwork at markets across Accra, as well as in Kumasi and Cape Coast. During that time, I have been an observant participant or interviewer of 103 porters and accompanied three women on their return journeys to the Northern, Savannah, and Oti Regions. This section focuses on a four-month photovoice praxis with fifteen porters at Makola Market. At that time, digital cameras were far less accessible and affordable. As a result, I distributed a dozen 35 mm cameras and two digital cameras for the project. We learned together about loading and unloading film, image composition, lighting, and the social politics of picture taking, regarding the photograph's subject, who or what is subjected to the photographer's gaze, and who the photographer is. Through photovoice, I learned about the sentiments of home, migration, immobility, love, anxiety, and aspirations. We loaded the cameras with film each week to shoot for the next few days. Usually on Fridays, I exchanged the exposed film for new rolls and took the film for development at a nearby photo studio. I always had the film developed in duplicate so one set could be distributed at Rawlings Park or Old Fadama.

Fifteen women took up photography, but there were always nonphotographing porters who took part in conversations about pictures when we met at Rawlings Park, the popular work and break spot for porters on the southern side of the market. Bulk items from large delivery trucks are loaded and unloaded in the park, and many porters work the streets surrounding the park to keep an eye out for trucks pulling in to be unloaded or loaded. Once parked, the height of the trucks confers shade from the sun, and head porters use old tires and discarded wooden pallets as seating areas between parked vehicles. The trucks also provide a sound barrier that lowers the din of surrounding market trade. We sat on the oversized tires abandoned in the car park each week to look through pictures.

Over the six months of participatory photography, the group created about one thousand pictures. Much to my embarrassment then, I did not find many photographs aesthetically pleasing or ethnographically rich during most meetups. And yet the images I thought the most banal were the pictures that consistently elicited the strongest reactions from the photographers, therefore exposing the shallowness of my expectations. Sometimes they were nudes of women with their partners. Other times there were twenty shots of the same aluminum pan taken at different angles throughout the day. Portraits frequently cut the tops off heads or disembodied limbs. There were also piles of photographs that archived the women's consumer desires, where the photographs functioned as visual shopping lists of items they hoped to buy.

Pictures as data are fraught because photographs are widely understood as evidentiary "proof" of an event (Mulla 2011). I was also anxious about making claims to images as an effective interpretive framework without the written word (Mead 2009). My initial reactions to participatory photography join the ranks of many scholars who write against utilitarian expectations of images as data and consumptive desires around aesthetic creativity (Poole 1997). When the photovoice aspects of my fieldwork waned after I had reached my budget limits, I realized, through a cascade of opposing logics, how my responses to the photographs were rooted in my "inability to fully reckon with the issue of reception" (Shankar 2020, 206). Despite their best efforts, visual methods cannot fully resolve the power differences in fieldwork relationships or fully refuse audiences' expectations (Poole 2005). The private and personal circulation of porters' photos did not guard their images against the "problem of pleasure" that Arjun Shankar (2020, 209) describes as a process of viewing that circumscribes the powerful with entitled curiosity and the marginal as objects of curiosity, irrespective of their positioning in front of or behind the camera. Colleagues and mentors regularly queried whether porters' pictures resembled the beautiful photographs showcased in the award-winning documentary *Born into Brothels*, which featured images created by the children of sex workers in India. When I bumped into artists at the photo lab, they repeatedly asked whether there would be a photo exhibition to showcase their work. In email exchanges, friends anticipated seeing the "amazing" pictures.

Although it is difficult to admit, I was dispassionate about most photographs' representational qualities and technical aspects. Rooted in believing that porters' photographs were inoculated from being fetishized as commodities because of how porters used pictures or talked about them, I almost missed how photos somatically marked experience and served as emotional placeholders. Aesthetics of images pushed me to reassess whose desires were centered in the method. The visual economy of photographs traced relationships, took note of desires, and were, sometimes, deliberately silent about tender contexts. Photographers made thoughtful decisions about which pictures to share with friends, save as keepsakes, or send to loved ones. The women who took part in photovoice generously gifted their time, but it was not without expectations for the photographs (and me) to also *do* certain things in return. We made care packages that included photos, which I sent to their natal communities by bus courier. Other times, women selected pictures to trade with each other as parting gifts for someone returning to their rural home.

For five years after photovoice, I did not earn permission to use photographs women had taken for academic research or publications. I had gained oral or written consent from each photovoice participant, but as institutional review board forms require and anthropologists acknowledge, there is also the reminder to participants that they can withdraw consent at any time. The photo lab manager where I developed the pictures asked for permission to use some of the photographs to advertise his services. When a friend asked about submitting pictures to the amateur exhibition at the Junior Arts Club, none of the women were interested in making a submission or allowing me to submit on their behalf. The women were serious about protecting their likenesses, especially as it became common for busloads of foreigners to tour the market and snap pictures of them wielding heavy loads. I have a small, curated collection of photographs a handful of women agreed to share outside the photovoice project, but people remain surprised that I have never held a fundraiser or exhibition of the photographs.

These outcomes are instrumental and informative for how researchers think about what methods signal and accomplish. As Joan Morgan observes, "when Black women's cultural products are read solely through a representation politic," the result "routinely discounts *black female interiority*" (2015, 37). I argue that my use of photovoice aids the reconciliation of fragmented desires and ruptured disappointments and uncovers the sensory "politic of articulation" in women's interior lives (Hammond 1997, 180). Photovoice as feminist method also exacted a revenge of consent that tested the ethics of care and trust between me and my interlocutors (Shankar 2020). Participation in photovoice and women's subsequent refusal to share pictures outside of the spaces where they lived and worked has a two-part result. Refusal, here, is the leveraging of trust in order for women to control who is entitled to gaze and who is gazed upon.[8] First, the conversations about photographs surveyed ontologies of porterage and visually rendered how women parsed the differences among the ways head-loading is imagined, perceived, embodied, and performed. Second, their refusal to share images outside of a space they take up insists that the joy of praxis exists in a higher value than the representation, reception, and circulation of the photographs. I interpret these generative rejections as forms of pleasure activism, which adrienne maree brown defines as "happiness, satisfaction, and enjoyment," as the essential components of efforts to "reclaim our whole, happy, and satisfiable selves from the impacts, delusions, and limitations of oppression and/or supremacy" (2019, 13). Pleasure activism exists in close kinship with Audre Lorde's (1984) uses of the erotic, whereby the fun of storytelling with, about, and alongside photographs reveals the hidden transcripts of work and leisure. Joy, refusal, and the erotic become theoretics that reject the dehumanizing foreclosure of emotional depth assigned to Black women. Whether taking shape in Rahida's refusal of photovoice but witty interjections during my conversations with people who did participate or details about sexual violence through metaphors about hair care and food, which I discuss next, creative methodologies do lend themselves to expressive sifting of intimacy and refusal that craft ethnography from below.

Kitchen Table Politics: Charcoal Pot Edition

Friday and Sunday were the best days to talk with women about whatever pictures they had taken in the weeks before. Muslim porters rarely porter after Friday afternoon prayer. Sundays are the most uninterrupted days of the week; sales occur languidly. Porters with enough money to cover their daily needs (bath and drinking water, fees for the public toilets, and food) tend to forgo the forty-minute walk to Makola. Most shops are closed, fewer traders set up their stalls, and fewer hawkers roam market roads to sell. On Sundays, the nearby settlements are more chill, as upbeat music blasts from every direction. Porters spend the day relaxing amid the variegated infrastructure that constitutes their chill spots, including an abandoned flat tire now operating as a chair or the shade conferred by the shadow of a parked Mack truck. The domestication of these mostly public spaces confers a semblance of privacy for porters to gather and pass the time.

Most Sundays, Balima, her roommates, and their friends sit outdoors on sleeping mats they lay on the ground in front of the tin-and-wood container they rent. The single room is too hot to sit comfortably inside during the day in the dry season. Outside, the ground is packed dry and flat, and a battery-operated radio is propped on a plastic chair with cracked legs. "I bore," said Fusena, speaking sluggishly to no one as she commanded the radio and intermittently changed stations to skip commercials and music and to search for talk shows to listen to. Zaa and A1 are Fusena's favorite stations, but the frequency of those savanna-based stations does not reach the capital, and there are no Accra-based stations that broadcast talk shows in languages Fusena speaks fluently. But in Sunday's tepid energy and languishing vibes, Fusena continued to surf radio stations, twirling the radio's knobs. Even if she found a talk show she liked, the conversation could hardly compete with the sound systems around the neighborhood.

Fusena's roommate Balima porters at Makola Market to raise money to stock her wedding trousseau. In her home community, a young woman shows her readiness for marriage with a complete supply of kitchenware, cooking supplies, and perhaps a few family heirlooms. Balima purchased a charcoal pot and aluminum stockpots a few weeks prior. Charcoal pots are an affordable and durable appliance found in most Ghanaian households, whether rural, urban, elite, or poor.[9] Coal pots come in various shapes and sizes but are typically rectangular, standing about a foot from the ground. They have an underlying tray that holds charcoal with a square funneled grate that allows ashes to fall into a three-walled compartment. The name is a slight misnomer, for it is not a pot at all but a metal stand that only requires charcoal, a bit of kerosene, wood, and a watchful eye to spark a fire and prepare a meal.

Coal pots are affordable and accessible, but most porters have neither the resources nor the time to cook regularly. This Sunday, Balima allowed us to fire up her new coal pot to cook a meal together. Someone quickly foraged for a pot among the neighbors; Balima was adamant about her shiny five-liter pot remaining untouched before it went to her marriage household. When someone prepares a Sunday meal, it is usually *tuo zaafi*, a starchy dish that comprises maize and water that accompanies a bitter-leaf, okra, or groundnut soup. During the week, Sakina, Balima, and Fusena drink Hausa *koko* for breakfast or buy food from Hajia Safia,[10] who sells *waakye* close to Abossey Okai Central Mosque. *Waakye*, made from black-eyed peas or red cowpeas, is a rice-and-bean dish boiled with dried sorghum leaves and *kanwa* (a salt-based seasoning like baking soda). An ancestor to hoppin' John, Jamaican rice and peas, and Guyanese cook-up, *waakye* is accompanied by a thick tomato-based stew, *wele* (softened and seasoned cow skin), boiled eggs, *shitor* (a fish-based hot pepper), and *taalia* (spaghetti noodles).

At least two *waakye* stalls are found in most Accra neighborhoods, and several can be passed from Old Fadama and Agbogbloshie to Rawlings Park. Ghana is always a contender in the playful "jollof wars," the social media rivalry about which country cooks up the most flavorful and appetizing jollof rice. Still, when it comes to *waakye*, sellers from northern Ghana are universally heralded as the best architects of the dish. Hajia Safia, whose modest green stall is tucked on a crumbling corner of Ring Road, is originally from Langa, a town in the Northern Region. She has sold *waakye* in Accra for the last twelve years. Sakina and her friends frequently take a six-minute detour to eat at Hajia Safia's, whose *waakye* is served near scalding with a generous pour-over of stew. The wooden stall is an open-back shed, painted red and white, with images of beans and fish painted in the front. Beside the shed are two benches where Hajia Safia's daughter sits at one end and washes emptied bowls in a basin of sudsy water.

Because the serving dishes are always clean, the seating area tidy, and the *wele* soft without being chewy, Hajia Safia's massive *waakye* pot sold out within two hours of sunrise prayer. I did not visit Old Fadama often, but whenever I told my assistant Esther about my plans for an early morning trip to the area, she accompanied me and stopped at Hajia Safia's. Everyone is chatty over a hearty breakfast, and more so when I'm buying. Barakesu calls Hajia Safia's *waakye* "sweet" like her sister's cooking that she misses from back home. After months of visits and curious cajoling, Hajia Safia shared a secret about her sorghum leaves, a central ingredient to the rice dish. Hajia Safia only buys the leaves from farmers who grow sorghum separate from corn. According to Hajia Safia, when sorghum grows close to maize, the corn stunts the growth of the sorghum leaves, which then diminishes the flavor of the leaves when they are dried and then added to the boiling water and rice.

This particular Sunday afternoon, we were cooking *kyinkaafa/shinkafa*.[11] An amalgamation of *waakye* and jollof, *shinkafa* is made with brown rice, dried or fermented fish, beans, tomatoes, onions, ginger, red pepper, and garlic. I bought the ingredients, Fusena borrowed a large pot from a friend, and my assistant Esther picked up charcoal, kerosene, beans, and spices. During visits to the settlement, Esther's companionship was more appropriate and welcomed than Solomon's for interacting with women in their personal living spaces.

Esther and I walked the eastern edges of Korle Lagoon; the scent of burning e-waste, kerosene, and pit latrines clung in the air.[12] The rows of tin rooms mostly house multigenerational and short- and long-term migrants and sit atop aluminum cans, discarded plastic bags, and flattened dried earth. During the rainy season, the ground swims with damp trash, but during this dry season day, the ground was so dry it could be tidily swept without creating dust.

It was well before dusk when Esther and I arrived at the metal storage unit where Sakina, Balima, Fusena, and five other women reside when in Accra. The mosquitoes were not feeding with force, but the stagnant water from the lagoon invited pests to hover. Only one window is cut into the structure to offer relief, but the temperature of the interior hangs above ninety-five degrees on a sunny day. The metal ten-by-ten-foot shipping container sharply contrasts with the coolness instilled by the clay and thatched compound houses of their hometowns. A single light bulb hangs from a cord in the ceiling. Four-foot-high cardboard barrels store personal items, and straw sleeping mats line the floor. The only other things in the space were the carrying pans propped beside the door. One of the pans was loaded with a bundle of wax-print fabric, a napping infant inside the concave bowl.

Four cement blocks lay sideways to form a staired entrance into the metal box. The wide-swing door was open, a lasso of sisal threaded through the padlock hole, the ends twisted around loosened metal on a corner drain hole. Above the threshold, a half yard of lace hangs over the entrance to catch any passing breeze. There is no internal locking mechanism, so when the door is pulled shut at bedtime, a pan is wedged under the U-shaped slide-lock handle. A heavy-duty padlock hangs open on the exterior, and everyone suspects the landlord holds the key so he can swiftly evict the group should they fall too far behind on the weekly rent. Rent money is pooled on Wednesdays to pay for the space. In some shacks, rent is set on a per-person, per-week basis. Everyone contributes what they can, when they can. Balima had no money, but she had bought everyone's bathing water from the nearby polytank.[13] Still feeling bad about not having money, Balima offered her coal pot for the meal preparation.

Confident that her meal would be as delicious as Hajia Safia's *waakye*, Sakina joked that we needed to call her Hajia Kina as she divided our meal-prep tasks. The steep time overhead of most days accentuates the decision of afternoon cooking.[14] A three-legged plastic chair is balanced against a concrete block that is a step into the container. Since it is broken, no one ever sits on it. After the fire was sparked, the coal pot sat to the left of the steps, and Hajia Kina cut ginger and pepper, using the chair seat as a cutting board. Fusena pulled a frond mat outdoors for seating. The plan to cook *shinkafa* gave this Sunday a more languid feel. I sat on the concrete step to cut onions and tomatoes. We passed the knife around until I remembered the Swiss Army knife in my bag. We set a black plastic bag on the ground to catch the vegetable refuse. Esther settled over the threshold with the voice recorder and cuddled with the awakening infant. The conversation came in spurts, flitting between chopping sounds and chatter. Cooking is a prerequisite to commensal care. Sunday is one of the few days porters rest or slowdown from head-loading. Still, what feels like autonomy in a surplus labor economy—cooking and eating together on a day off—renders the most basic act of sustenance a labor expense.

I named this section "Kitchen Table Politics: Charcoal Pot Edition" to hold space for the tools that made cooking meals together possible. I also did this to note how a charcoal pot and the activities surrounding it transformed a dusty space into a place where self-fashioning through commensality is taken seriously. Domestic spaces such as kitchens have long been a place of interest for understanding how social relations are fostered, and close consideration has been given to kitchens as a sphere of socialization into gender roles, both liberatory and oppressive (Hanrahan 2015). In African and African-descendant homeplaces,[15] the kitchen is a transformed site that offers a respite from the hardship of grueling labor demands. In African American English, "the kitchen" is also the tight curls located at the nape of the neck. The kitchen is where Black women do each other's hair, because of the actual kitchen's attributes of heating elements needed to hot-comb hair or the sink for rinsing someone else's hair. Both of these kitchens are preeminent venues for sense-work, from the haptic bond between scalp and womanhood to the tactile and olfactory aliveness of hair-care intimacy (Omotoso 2018; hooks 1989). The kitchen, as well as around the kitchen table, is where inner thoughts become outwardly expressed in stories that artfully acquiesce and intermittently disrupt the precarious norms of the service-labor economy and its ties to the projects of modernity and postcoloniality (Tamale 2020).

On a different Sunday afternoon, the three-legged chair / cutting board we used to dice ingredients became a hairdressing station. When I arrived at the container that day, Balima had just fetched three gallons of water in the ubiquitously repurposed yellow plastic oil jugs. A purple box of Dark and Lovely Triple Silkening Relaxer was unboxed on the concrete step. The cellophane gloves pressed into the paper accordion of instructions were draped over the arm of the chair. The directions on how to chemically straighten, or "relax," hair are outlined in English, Spanish, Chinese, and French. Still, the paper is discarded, but not because of the linguistic inaccessibility of the instructions for porters. For most relaxed-hair veterans, the steps of execution are consistent, irrespective of brand.

1. Protective measures to keep the scalp from burning (Vaseline—check)
2. Gloves (check)
3. Water (gallon jugs—check)
4. Moisturizing conditioner (came in the kit—check)
5. Shampoo for the second wash (a square of Key soap—check)
6. Rat-tail comb (check)[16]
7. Protective cape draped around the shoulders (towel draped over Amena's shoulders—check)

Amena stays in the wooden lean-to down the lane and on the opposite side to Balima's. She moves between the shacks and the sleeping corners of the market to save money. This Sunday, she sat on the rolled mat and twirled the rat-tail comb while waiting for the straightening process to start.

As she handed me a jar of petroleum jelly, Balima said, "I'm too tired," as she lowered herself onto the mat beside Amena. Balima took a long, full-body stretch, then curled her hands under her chin, yawning as she settled beside Amena, who then looked at me expectantly. I immediately recognized this repertoire of Black womanhood, "understood the assignment," stepped behind Amena, and began to make crosswise parts in Amena's hair with the rat-tail comb. I hadn't straightened my hair in over twenty years, and I wore my hair in locs, but I was presumed to know how to do this work. They weren't wrong. As I finished greasing Amena's scalp and worked the sticky pomade around and behind her ears, Balima rolled on her side, reaching for the Dark and Lovely. We worked in easy quietness even though the chatter of music and work from the settlement surrounded us. Balima poured the no-lye activator into the larger jar of cream. She placed the lid back on the jar and shook the mixture vigorously. I wiped the excess Vaseline on the edges of the towel. Amena pulled the gloves from the arm of the chair, dangled them over her shoulder, and dropped them into my hand. I accepted them without protest, even though I was nervous.[17] I began to comb the straightening cream into the base of Amena's hair. Balima was outstretched on the sleeping mat, lamenting a tight ache in her neck. "It hurts too bad," she said as she kneaded her neck and shoulder.

Amena nodded sympathetically. "The pain is the price for carrying someone else's shit for hours," she replied.

I worked quietly as the women talked, thinking about the requests for Tiger Balm, Vicks VapoRub, and arnica cream I've fulfilled over the years. The topical salves were a small relief for muscle aches and joint pains. I lightly touched the crown of Amena's head and her shoulder. She dropped her chin toward her chest.

"You know the night watchmen around Tudu?" asked Amena, referring to the hired security men who patrol the warehouses through the night. "Of all the rapists, they are the most brutal."

Taken aback, I froze for a minute before asking, "All the rapists?"

"Yeah, the night watchmen. Rapists. All of them," Amena replied before quickly asking, "You get my ears?" Amena's head is tilted to the right, her neck uncomfortably angled toward her chin. This peek into her pain as a witness or survivor is folded in the practicalities of the moment. The haptics of hairstyling and the familiarity of the perming process dictate working from the back of the head (at the proverbial "kitchen") to the front. Amena's sharing about the violence of sexual assault at the end of the preparatory process matters. Amena's admonitive request about her ears seeks bodily protection in the motions of hair care. Her dialogic flip between the pains nested in an offhand comment and immediate hyperfocus to the practical application of hair grease is a critique of my surprise and a reflection of her psychic numbing energies. The metaphorical turn to protect her scalp opens toward and moves through the pains of vulnerability silenced by her need to make it through another day.

Amena and I had seen each other every day the previous week. We spent Friday in a group conversation about a recent batch of photos where one of the most striking images was of a sleeping *susu*[18] collector with feet dangling from the window of the roadside booth.

Amena asked, "Remember the *susu* one?" referring to her photograph of the collector's feet languishing over a brightly painted yellow *susu* sign. While porters hustled with head loads to earn money in order to contribute to the savings plan, the collector himself spent most of the day at rest. Amena added that when there isn't enough money to rent a space in a container, lean-to, or another shelter, send money home to care for her family's daily needs, *and* save money, she gathers with other women porters to sleep atop their metal pans with their belongings stuffed under the overturned lids. They sometimes huddle in the entryway of a closed shop or form a semicircle on the sidewalk of a quiet street. Amena explained that the larger the group, the less likely the harm. "Four is a good number," she added, but even still, it is common for "a boozed man" to pass by and verbally or physically attack someone as they sleep. Amena rested her face in her palm as I put on the plastic gloves from the box and mixed the activator and relaxer cream in a plastic bowl. Amena looked down and away.

"This guy holding my money, he dey chill [is relaxing]. But me, I have to think about some idiot tearing at my clothes, so I can give this guy something for my savings 'morrow."

Amena sucked her teeth—the quintessential gesture of knowing that moves between ordinary Black women (Shange 2019).[19] The bodily expression or sound are not easily translatable to language standards, but the gesture still narrates what Amani Morrison (2018, 84) describes as "black hair haptics," the polysemic registers of meanings articulated between Black women, and especially on hair days.

Porter work is a literal and symbolic struggle against systemic downward mobility, its experiences offering repetitive lessons on the cyclical and expansive nature of unbelonging and exclusion. Despite the recurrent violence of vulnerable sleeping arrangements, harm, and the sex differentiations of porter work, Amena's interior negotiations unfurl inside the calm of a restful day and lend to stillness as knowing and affirmation. The time together, in the kitchen, however fleeting, untangles the spatial and discursive tensions of hypervisibility and invisibility. Conversation in the calm and quiet[20] oppose the routinized assaults of work, and extend beyond the traders, hawkers, shopkeepers, truck drivers, and security personnel, who each play a part in how much money Amena and others can earn. The refuge of hair care makes space for Amena to sift trauma without lurid evidentiary details. In her metaphorical and inward-focused commentary, the specifics are not necessary to lay bare in order to validate her feelings.

CHAPTER 4

=====

Queering Polygamy

All of us have a role to play in imagining, and perhaps
enacting, new possibilities for human society.

—Leith Mullings

The lantern's flame flickered in the crosswind of conversation. After a satisfying meal, a thick yam soup made from dried fish and hot pepper, Tani wandered toward Barakesu, me, and a few others, all of whom relaxed on a frond mat.

"Fine evening," greeted Barakesu as Tani approached.

Cross-legged and wrapped in a brown-and-green batik, Barakesu patted a space beside her.

"Sit and tell something," said Barakesu as she motioned her right arm toward Tani. Tani smiled at the invitation, lowering herself to the ground. As she wiggled her hips into the mat for steady comfort, Barakesu's knee affectionately knocked Tani's crossed legs. With her shoes discarded two paces before stepping onto the frond, Barakesu pulled the corner of the green-and-brown batik cloth across both of their shoulders.

"Husband is good?" asked Barakesu.

"Hmmm," affirms Tani, confirming that she called home earlier in the day.

"The children?" asked Barakesu.

"They are all fine," replied Tani.

Barakesu (or Kesu, for short) and Tani are in their early to mid-twenties. They are married to Yohance, who lives near Bimbila with their first wife, Baiwa.

When I first learned about their shared husband, I boldly asked, "Is he rich?"

Without missing a beat, Barakesu quipped, "In kindness."

There are three reasons I was surprised to learn that Barakesu and Tani were married to the same man. First, Barakesu and Tani were both in their twenties at the time of our conversations, and polygamy is increasingly uncommon among young people in Ghana. Second, among most young adults in Accra, "polygamous" was an often-used derisive or celebratory moniker attached to men who maintained sexual relationships with multiple women. Third, during these initial years of ethnographic research, I knew Tani and Barakesu as domestic partners, a same-gender couple, not as co-wives of a polygamous household. My understanding was not an inference or assumption deduced from the loving way they called each other "my wife" or their demonstrated affections. Across the course of several months, we had had regular conversations about the sexual-identity naming and politics they attached (and did not attach) to their relationship. And until that particular evening where we sat enjoying a breezy respite from dry season heat, Tani and Barakesu had never mentioned a marriage.

"Married?" I asked. The breeze slowed, as if on cue, and the lantern shone steady and bright across all of our faces. Barakesu's dispassionate gaze complemented Tani's shrug and half smile. Sitting side by side, Tani and Barakesu were incuriously posed, their colorful batik giving more energy than their gaze. Their relaxed expressions and cool posture reminded me of Rahida's earlier rejections, a barely perceptible signal that more *there* was there and that quiet curiosity was now required.

Barakesu and Tani's comfort in refusing to register my surprise was punctuated by the rhythmic side-to-side sway of their bodies with the cool breeze. Their mild emotive drips of humor were laced with being "unbothered and above concern."[1] Tani lazily rocked from left to right. The pause clung to the air in apt attunement to the languid energy of the evening. Barakesu's nonreactive posture was not without feeling; she was just unfazed by our surprise. Tani hummed a tune with a soft whistle that coaxed and teased her. Just before the pause inched into uncomfortable silence, Barakesu cleared her throat and said, "Listen, listen."

The Poor Farmer with Three Wives

"I was to marry Daáre, Yohance's brother. My parents knew his people. Many years ago, our fathers worked in the timber region together, and there was a joke-not joke that the children would marry. I saw him [Daáre] a few times. The guy [Daáre] looked nice [handsome], so when our parents chose to do this thing [the betrothal], I didn't mind. Daáre was hardworking. And because everyone knew we were getting married, I sometimes visited him on this cocoa farm near Oti, where he worked. The place was nice and peaceful," said Barakesu, her voice taking on a singsong rhythm. Esther translated in the spaces between Barakesu's reverie.

Barakesu continued. "He was sending money, taking care of things here and there, and getting ready [for marriage]. And then, nothing."[2] For a few weeks, no one was too worried. Sometime after that, someone came to the village asking for the repayment of money Daáre had borrowed. The visitor said Daáre had been away from working at the farm for over a month.

"After that, there was so much gossip," said Barakesu. In one rumor, a neighbor felt certain that Daáre was the unidentified pedestrian killed in a car accident on the N9 / Tamale-Yendi Road. When Yohance, Daáre's older brother, went to seek answers, he met with a man who said he was Daáre's friend. The friend also worked at the farm and said Daáre along with two other men had borrowed money to travel the Sahara into Libya to cross the Mediterranean into Italy for work. The friend said Daáre didn't tell the family because he didn't want them to worry. Yohance was unconvinced by this story but relieved that the unidentified pedestrian was not his brother. Either way, Daáre was gone, leaving his family in grief and disbelief. On a more practical note, the family had given a bride token (a symbolic version of a bride-price, or bridewealth) to Barakesu's father, but the sorrow surrounding Daáre's absence kept most of those conversations at bay.

During this same period, Yohance struggled on the family farm. Yohance was the only farmer in the area to have a soybean contract with a European investor, and his decision to grow the cash crop had spoiled relations with neighbors. In the end, that period's harvest had a better yield than the previous one, but it was not enough to support hiring additional workers. Yohance, Baiwa (the first wife), and their new wife, Tani, all wanted their children to spend more time in school than at work on the land, so Baiwa and Tani encouraged Yohance to marry Barakesu. An emblematic face-saving gesture more than a consummated one, this marriage allowed the families to keep convivial relations, maintain hope for Daáre's return, and avoid repayment of the bride token. The symbolic marriage also cajoled Barakesu's eldest brother into joining their household because of its proximity to the high school. Baiwa agreed to look after the children when the pair was away and ensured that the necessary payments for uniforms and school supplies were made.

In addition to the marital unit, the agricultural household includes Barakesu's brother and six children. On the farm, they grow yams and guinea corn (sorghum). The increasing unreliability of the rainy season and crop yield has led to greater food insecurity. Two years ago, Baiwa, Barakesu, and Tani had discussed porter work as a financial supplement to tide the family over between planting and harvest. After a few family meetings, it was decided that Barakesu and Tani would porter together; both came to porter in Accra.

"We are all focused on the children's future," said Tani, whose cherub face signaled she was on the cusp of adulthood. An ingenue, perhaps; since age estimates coalesce around events and birth order rather than dates, each household parent is under thirty yet they are all steadfast in their financial commitments to the schooling of the youngest members of the household.

Inching closer to Tani, Barakesu added, "And I get more time to enjoy my wife more more," doubling her words to express her pleasure. Esther blushed and cast her eyes downward in shyness at the innuendo of enjoyment. This was the first pause in translating that Esther had taken since Tani and Barakesu began to speak. After another break, Tani chimed in, with a tenor of dramatic folklore, "And this . . . is how Yohance, a poor man . . . came to have three wives."

Polygamy is uncommon in Bikpakpaam communities; more than two spouses are rarer still, yet Tani and Barakesu are Yohance's second and third wives, respectively. Tani had been married to Yohance for four years at the time of this conversation. Barakesu is the widow of Yohance's brother, who mysteriously disappeared while away at work in the Oti Region. Tani and Barakesu are close in age and guess there are about ten years between them and their first wife. The family has six children.

Yohance is the patrilineal steward of the land, and Barakesu married in for her children to retain access to farming in the area.

"Every land is someone's land. You have to have land in order to build a house," said Tani. The shrinking harvests and dwindling income persist, but so does Barakesu and Tani's commitment to land entitlements. With all of Yohance's siblings away from the area and working in the mining and forestry sectors, the practicalities of an old-school marriage creatively render possibilities for planning different futures.

"Do they know? What do they think?" asked Esther about Baiwa and Yohance.

"They know," said Tani.

"They don't mind," Barakesu added.

"And if they do?" asked Tani, touching Kesu's wrist.

Tani shrugged.

"Well! If they know, they know. But they don't come around, and they don't take care of us, soooo . . ." said Tani, her voice trailing off.

"They can challenge us, but it won't work," said Barakesu. "Our children, the boys *and the girls*, go to school. We're getting somewhere, somehow."

"Ghana is sweet, but money matters is bitter. Here in Accra and at home," said Tani.

"Nobody cares that we sleep with our arms and legs together," Barakesu said, squeezing Tani's arm and still folding her in a hug. "They may even bring words against us, but we are the ones who buy the food that gives them the strength to open their mouths to talk." Barakesu's thumb softly brushed each of Tani's fingertips.

"And I work hard," said Barakesu as she continued to tenderly count Tani's fingers.

"I love my wife, our children, the man, and my wife," her fingers tracking each love.

Tani leaned in closer to Barakesu, emphasizing, "Annnnd, we are also very humble," smiling as she took a cleansing, meditative breath before resting her face on Barakesu's shoulder.

"Still," said Esther poetically, "romance without finance is a nuisance." We all nodded. Whether the affirmation was simple acknowledgment of words spoken or agreement with the sentiment was unclear.

South African literary scholar, feminist, and poet Danai Muposta asks, "When will African women get to study interiorities" without enduring criticism that they have displayed "self-indulgence and privilege?" (2010, 3). In a similar vein, Kenyan queer feminist scholar Neo Sinoxolo Musangi calls for more work like Ifi Amadiume's (1987) research on flexible gender roles and matricentric relationships in Nigeria that privilege "the how—rather than the what" of gender and sexuality through commitments that write "against the veiling of processes of knowledge production" (Musangi 2018, 404). As a contribution to this discourse, this chapter opens with the way Tani and Barakesu love on each other in order to center interiority and care as the essential adhesives for spousal and parental capacities.

From professional relationships to personal interactions, listeners often distill conversations through the lens of their own personal understanding or experience with the matter at hand. In academia, scholars are quick to filter a project through the lens of their own perception of a place, so much so that they are unwilling to let people walk them through their own analytics. And this is no criticism of Esther's quip, but an effort to share the sense-work of mutual understanding around intimacy and partnerships, how women know each other through a range of sentiments that are internally felt but also recognized and affirmed. Resonant with the way Black feminists conceive of care as self-love and the community practice of generating power and agency, Barakesu and Tani leverage relationship agency at multiple registers (Finch 2022). Tani's assertion of humility and Esther's comment blend labor and marriage as "a love made visible" to push against the notion that love needs nothing but love (Aidoo 1977, 41). The ability to fulfill financial responsibilities and buttress their household precarity helps sustain their relationship. As far as Tani was concerned, criticisms about her life choices were muted by the material benefits of her and Barakesu head-loading and living together. Tani said, "People can 'talk,' but anyone whose mouth she feeds" cannot speak against her.

Shifts in the household agency, informed by the death of a fiancé, reduced crop yields, and who is expected to earn money or keep house signals toward compulsory heteronormativity, but these factors do not undermine or deter how Barakesu and Tani cobble together a rich day-to-day life to meet their needs. Their self-fashioned queering of polygamy reconstructs a sustaining livelihood, in what Kirk Fiereck, Neville Hoad, and Danai Muposta describe as "lineaments of the queer customary" (2020, 364), a temporal body politic that rearticulates intergenerational norms into a generative response to precarity. Similar to Keguro Macharia's (2019, 23) interest in the "banal fact" of embodiment and what the ordinary can reveal, Kesu and Tani's belonging to each other and their "sweet like sugar" intimacies thrive on sediments of ambivalence. Therefore, rather than delineate precisely what queerness, as a category, does or does not accomplish on behalf of the care economy among head porters in Accra (Spronk and Nyeck 2021), my use of queering polygamy is a lens to see how liberatory possibilities come forth in same-gender relationships that include sexual and nonsexual habits of attention and affection (Sekyiamah 2022). Also, while the term *queer* is not used by any of the women, their experiences reject polygamy as a wholesale manifest of cisheteropatriarchy worth considering more seriously (Whitehouse 2023).[3] This chapter traverses the bittersweet flexibilities of marriage and the counterprivates of sexuality that come into being through subtle enactments, avoidances, and expressions. Queering polygamy, as a form of sense-work, reveals how women make homeplaces, craft privacy in semipublic spaces, and nurture the necessary discernments to survive habitual poverty and momentarily thrive in a climate of chaotic displacement.

A disruption to the "hegemonic ways in which 'queer' Others have been called into being" (Dankwa 2021, 8), as well as the manner and methods through which relational intimacies are narrated about African women, queering polygamy aligns with the way Africans are queered as "the Other to European/Western modernity" (Otu and van Klinken 2023, 514). In that vein, it is not far-fetched to find queerness in African ethnography. However, cisheteropatriarchy casts queerness and blackness as foibles of the "savage slot" (Trouillot 2003) to legitimate capitalism, coloniality, and slavery as necessities of the modern nation-state (Mampane 2022). In the hermeneutics of the suffix -*ness* I mentioned in Chapter 2, blackness and queerness, then, are categories of the subhuman or nonhuman (Jackson 2020) that render Black queer people as static and staid objects of observation.

This chapter pushes against queerness as another metaphor for deviance and disposability (Nhemachena and Warikandwa 2019) and focuses on queerness as a anti-hegemonic normalcy that "disturbs the order of things" (Ahmed 2006, 161). Tani and Barakesu's marriage rejects the narrative of impossibilities sutured to the lives of African women, and their experiences highlight how families maintain cohesive relationships against the corrosive conditions of divestment and dispossession. Their story is a through line to intimate relationships that adds complexity to the ethnographic excesses of

African polygyny as wholesale gendered oppression.[4] Their partnerships are about the sociality of reciprocity, sensual habits, and work, all of which yield greater safety and survivability for them. Moving beyond the suffering subject gives way for the mercurial nature of relationships and their material and affective improvisations. Ethnographic witness of the queer underpinnings of Barakesu and Tani's relationship will not topple the structures that inform their decisions, but their experiences do upend the complicities of heteronormativity.

The autonomies of Black women, especially African women who are poor, often go unrecognized and are rarely registered as possible. But bodily autonomy is the agency to make certain choices; for Tani, Barakesu, and some of the other women I discuss in this chapter, autonomy contours how emotional bonds are supported through a cascade of interactions. Tani and Barakesu queer polygyny through care as a form of infrastructure.[5] Infrastructure is often thought of in terms of physical sites, but it is also the sensework of tactile knowledges and gustatory sentiments of social connections. Shrewd improvisations and embodied affect do not substantively change the emotional bottlenecks that squelch optimism and hope, but empathy remains against the impasses of ordinary life (Berlant 2011). For Barakesu and Tani, the city and head-loading are a relational beard that affords a less surveilled intimate life.[6] Their queering of polygyny blends the "cathartic possibilities" of multiple marriages with the pleasures of sensual joy and life satisfaction (Arjona 2017, 54). For others, like Fusena and Sakina, discussed later in this chapter, bodily autonomy exists in the fleeting sanctuary of a temporary shelter, where women have physical space to detail the cruelty of social dictates and their frustration with class politics.

*   *   *

On our evening walk to the main road after our conversation with Barakesu and Tani, Esther and I never slowed when we reached our usual spot to say goodbye. The makeshift bus stop is where we usually make plans for our next meeting, hail cabs, and part ways. Hawking taxis and *trotros* passed, but Esther and I were too hyped in our processing of the conversation we just had with Tani and Barakesu to close out our time together.

"Two years, two years," I incredulously repeated.

"We've known these two for two years, and this is the first time they have everrrrr said anything," Esther chortled. "Of course, there was always the little hugs, tender touching, and their 'my wife, my wife' statements, but that's just how we Ghanaians are, always indirect, never by force." Shaking her head, Esther added, "We are always soooo . . ." (her voice trailing off).

"Ambiguous?" I asked.

"Exactly," said Esther, her moment of introspection slowing her pace to a stop. Squarely facing me, she empathically added, "Bey, you know, that is precisely the point."[7] Esther's comment about the point refers to Tani and Barakesu and the dynamics of our relationship. Esther and I talked about our conversation with Tani and Barakesu and our shared community of "not-straight" people who have shown up in fieldwork and friendships with blurry relationship statuses and sexual identities. Our quick calculations estimated that more than one hundred hours of conversation and time had been spent with Barakesu and Tani over the previous two years. We were surprised, but not shocked, at how much time had passed before we learned about their relationship and unique family dynamics.[8]

A tapestry of emotional intimacy is woven into the conversations Barakesu, Esther, Tani, and I had over the years, from interviews and photo-voice meetings to jocular ribaldry and chatter about our children. Barakesu and Tani express relentless appreciation for their senior wife's care, evidenced in their pride about all their children attending school. Once, Esther laughed uproariously when Barakesu asked whether *supi[lesbian]* was the same as the English word *soup*; the sexual innuendo and image of bringing a bowl to one's mouth to drink soup was a multilingual wordplay. On another occasion, while swirling a spoon in a cup of tea, Tani wistfully described her sex life as "sweet like sugar."

A taxi driver honked and waved his hands, interrupting the rhythm of Esther's and my stroll. I stopped and halfheartedly haggled over the taxi fare until Esther suggested that we continue to walk and talk. In the same way that Esther and I slowed our pace to reminisce and process our earlier conversation, I need to make an ethnographic detour here to write about my relationship with Esther to explain its overlapping significance with the conversation we had with Barakesu and Tani.

Esther and I have been friends and collaborators for nearly twenty years. In addition to her work as my research assistant and translator, I am close friends with Esther and her partner, Sami.[9] Sami and Esther work for trans-national organizations, and their work takes them across Europe, Africa, and North America. Both women are Ghanaian nationals from upper-class fam-ilies with multiple-entry visas or dual citizenship in Europe and the United States. They enjoy enviable global mobility, yet the couple has committed to spending at least three months of the year together in Ghana, residing in their secretly owned apartment in Accra. Both women identify as "not straight" to close friends. Esther explained how she "sort of came out to one of her sib-lings and a cousin, when [she] corrected them for calling Sami 'her room-mate.'" Sami often tells stories about her mother's "grave concern" for "her daughter, the spinster." In 2008, when I was having dinner with Esther and Sami, years before they began their relationship, Esther remarked that my basic knowledge of Twi coupled with a male research assistant who only spoke southern languages would be "a non sequitur; project dead in the water." I was embarrassed and hurt by Esther's comment,[10] but I appreciated her can-dor. When Esther offered to work as my research associate when our Accra dates coincided, I accepted her generous offer. Esther identifies as "a proud northerner" when referencing her family's multiethnic and multilinguistic tapestry of identities and language competencies. Because of this background, coupled with her advanced degree in comparative literature, Esther was eager to apply her knowledge to a project in Ghana. We have been friends, col-leagues, collaborators, and self-described coconspirators ever since.

I assemble narratives oriented by the knowledges of the people with whom I have community. Attentiveness to relationships rejects the idea that casual interactions are anecdotes that lack data. Stories can cogently detail power differentials and their varied impacts on the lives of the people we work alongside (Bolles 2020). This story also makes plain the ways in which translation and transcription muddle participatory ethics, especially when ethnographers strive to be less extractive or counter the stereotype of the lone (often male), "objective" researcher (Harrison 2016). My relationship with Esther is an instructive affirmation of the value of long-term friend-ship, not as evidence of being a good anthropologist with strong relation-ships with "informants" but for how to approach our interlocutors, and their criticism, with a seriousness and humility that considers fieldwork flexible and ongoing. Barakesu, Esther, Tani, and I came to an intersubjective space of stories that reveal how people negotiate constraints they have limited control over. Narratives have information about the agency of intimacies to shape the stories we tell, which in turn determines how those narratives are structured. My friendship with Esther also shows how, and the degree to which, methods matter in the way we collect information. Global mobility confers socioeconomic flexibilities on Esther and Sami's lives, but transnational privilege is a thin armament against homophobia.

Barakesu and Tani's marriage engenders educational opportunities for their children, but it does not fully dismantle the gendered expectations of care or influence how fruitfully crops grow. Resilience is a coping strategy rather than a virtue (Williams 2018), and it does well to explore how insights about precarity and suffering come forth through emotional and sensory knowledges of same-gender intimacy. Rather than simply extolling survivability, stories orient us to the creative improvements people make in their lives.

Day Breaks

Reggae nights at Akuma Village are lively and loud, despite the outdoor nightclub's location in the middle of a Ga neighborhood and wedged between the beach and Kwame Nkrumah Memorial Park. On the nights I partied late, I walked to Kinbu Gardens or Tema Station to visit porters before heading home. Although porters save money by not paying weekly rent in the Agbogbloshie residential area, the morning routine is financially and emotionally costly for women who sleep outdoors. Sallow skies blush over women awakening atop overturned pans to queue at the water tap. There, they might purchase a dollop of *alata samina* or a tear of sisal before constructing a makeshift shower near a gutter to wash up for the day. The fabric that usually serves as a head cushion sometimes serves as a drying towel before women get dressed for work.

Charcoal darkness gives way to flaxen daybreak. When I piggyback visiting porters at this early/late hour, I am unaccompanied by research assistants to translate, which prescribes with whom I can chat.[11] Behind the lottery stand, I buy porridge and *bofrot* before circling back to the beach near the arts center or the nook under the stairs at the car park. The heat from the porridge and donuts steams the inside of the black polyethylene bag. My arrival with breakfast eases the time and money pressures of the morning routine. Whether women have water for bathing is determined by whether they had slept indoors or outside, worked overnight, recently sent money home, or had good earnings from the day before. The women who porter at Rawlings Park chat a bit longer when breakfast is delivered.

Sitting around this morning were Ajara, Amena, Tani, and Barakesu, all women in their late teens or early twenties who portered at Rawlings Park and participated in the photo projects. When I arrived at the car park, Ajara was detailing the rowdy atmosphere at Tema Station's night market and a *trotro* passenger's intervention in an argument between the driver and a chocolate malt seller. Everyone worked as they talked. Ajara pulled her freshly washed and dried shirt from a woodpile. Tani drank *koko* [porridge] as Barakesu tore the breakfast bread. I peeked at Amena, and we shyly smiled at each other before focusing our gaze back on Ajara.

A few hours earlier, there was an embarrassing pause when Amena and I ran into each other in an alley behind Assase Pa restaurant. At the end of the lane that snaked in front of Akuma Village, I sat with a group of Rastas smoking weed on a semicircle of logs around a fire. Just a short walk from the majestic Kwame Nkrumah Memorial Park and the venerated Accra Arts Centre, a lane of wood stalls sat parallel to the ocean. Amena trailed slightly behind a man who had just exited the barely private rooms rented for sex work. Amena wore a black, slim-cut formfitting dress and a curly-cut Cleopatra-style wig. I passed the spliff to my right, and the man cut left down another alley as Amena and I made eye contact across the glow of the fire. Bound in embarrassment, we did not greet one another. Now, hours later, we shared a conspiratorial glance as we chatted with the women sheltered at a woodpile near the Timber Market entrance. Everyone else was either bathing or brushing their teeth. I wore jeans with tree bark stains dusting the backside, and Amena wore a maxi-length floral skirt over her black dress, the lace trim at the neckline accentuating her collarbones. Since we last saw one another, Amena had also added a button-down paisley shirt that was half buttoned and tucked into her skirt's waistband. Her hair was still pinned under a stocking cap. I wondered where she had stored her wig.

Sex work and smoking weed are illegal and feel even more illicit at the dawn of a workday, even though people regularly engage in both. The governing regimes of the surplus-labor economy demand constant improvisations in service work, which require multivalent efforts to stave off diminishing income. Outdoor sleep spaces regularly have the energy of places that operate twenty-four hours a day. Morning chatter is like shift reports at a hospital or gas station, where night workers recap notable events or issue warnings about the persistent issues that day-shift workers should expect.

Ajara dipped the half-cut water-bottle-turned-bathing-cup into the bucket as she asked Amena if the drinking spot had been busy the night before. Amena replied, "Nothing much happening." This acknowledgment of presence at bars, as well as vagueness about sex work, drinking, or weed, was a common admission about the self that also avoids judgments about other people's behaviors. Amena complained about the growing popularity of pre-scription painkillers at a nearby night pharmacy to divert attention away from herself.

At intermittent periods, the friends talk about alcohol, drugs, and sex. The stories women tell about themselves, and close friends focus on money earned, money owed, who was on the work scene, and whether their vibes were cool. There are occasional warnings or lamentations about how much money is spent on leisure, but, whether in reference to porterage or other forms of labor like sex work, Amena and Barakesu frequently say, "Work is work." In corners-corners,[12] however, there are no hierarchical social valuations or moral judgments about how people make money, just whether they have any. Every porter I know theorizes how money matters through the measure of time spent and whether the result has reciprocal or financial benefit (Win 2009).

Located near the Accra General Post Office and Melcom Supermarket on Pagan Road, City Car Park garage opened in 2007 and is within easy walk-ing distance to the courts, the center of Makola, and the Accra Arts Centre. The indoor garage has three levels of parking and is one of the few covered parking decks in the central business district. Within six months of its open-ing, power surges from load shedding short-circuited the automated pay station, which was subsequently replaced by a single-occupancy pay booth near the exit by Standard Chartered Bank. To the left of the ground-floor pedestrian entrance, a barrier of orange cone blocked one of the three stairwells.

The heavy downpours of the rainy season severely clogged the drains on the top deck, and the overflow poured steadily from the top of the build-ing. A secondary beam needed to be retrofitted to shore up the structural integrity of the garage against water damage. Because the area was closed off, the parking attendant engaged in light surveillance of the area, with most of his attention focused on the cars parked on the ground level. Vehicles usually departed well before the garage closed at six o'clock.

During the shift change, the parking attendant was relieved by an evening guard. Most nights that I saw him, the guard had removed the chair from the pay booth, propped it against the interior wall in a way that provided a view of all the entrances and exits, and napped. Some nights we greeted each other, and others, we both pretended not to see each other as I walked the outdoor perimeter of the garage and stepped over the damp, crumbly mound of the side entrance.

A nook beneath the stairway is camouflaged by its odd angle just out of the line of sight of the night guard. The tangle of access further isolates the spot. If someone chose to leave the garage at the side of the deck near those stairs, the driver exited onto a one-way street that headed deeper into the dense market traffic rather than away from it.

Fusena was the first to settle in the spot, followed by Sakina and Ajara, who usually take midday naps in the space before roaming for costumers during the evening rush hour. Fusena explains how she noticed the space underneath the stairs one day when a woman stiffed her after she had carried a big load to the garage.

"I was on the road to roam a bit when I spied this Accra lady. She was looking so clean, in white clothes and dark shades. She had come to do some serious shopping because she was holding a paper list. Also, no bags yet and nobody following, I know she was just starting." Fusena ditched her plans to go to the interior of Makola and fell in step a few paces behind the woman, her pan tipped sideways in subtle advertisement of her availability.

Tani stood at the curb, acting as part of the scene. Tilting her face skyward, Tani pantomimed pulling sunglasses from her face and looked toward Fusena. Fusena put her hands on her hips and waved her face with her right hand before giving the nonverbal flick of the wrist imitating the Accra lady's acceptance of Fusena's offer of services. Tani walked an empty parking space like a runway model, sashaying and pointing at imaginary shopping items. She walked down the parking space and back before returning to her space on the curb and motioning for Fusena to continue. Everyone laughed at Tani's reenactment before returning their attention to Fusena, who said, "And so I work and wait." Ajara giggled in anticipation. The story had been told several times before; the laugh foreshadowing the forthcoming anger and pain.

"I'm close but not too close," said Fusena. "Some people walk small, buy plenty, and leave fast. But this one, she is taking her time. Carrots. Pineapples. Each time she pays, I lower my pan and say, 'Madam' to her as the seller places her things in my pan. I can tell she likes the respect. I bend down something like eight times. Eight times, I give a 'Please, madam' to my customer. I get customer so I follow am [them]. Cool."

Counting off on her fingers, Fusena said, "She bought plenty things. Cabbage, pepper, fish, tomatoes, chocolate, bread." At some point, Accra lady looks at a watermelon. "I'm thinking, 'This thing no go-go' [won't fit in the pan]. If she calls somebody else to help, this money is going down. But, whew, she read my mind and did not buy, *al-hamdulillah* [thank God]. When she finished, we come here," said Fusena, looking widely around the car park.

"I had never been inside this place. Fresh building. The place is cool and quiet be. We walk to the car. It's nice, so clean and shiny," she said admiringly. Tani stretched her legs out and motioned that she was holding an imaginary steering wheel.

"No dirt anywhere, you hear me? So okay, I'm set," Fusena added, in an excited conclusion that her compensation will match the manicured presentation of her customer. Ajara shook her head at the misfortunate calculation by rolling her eyes.

Fusena continued.

"So, she opens the back and I take down my pan. I load the things." Tani stood again, lifting imaginary items. "I place them there, fine-fine," said Fusena as Tani patted the air.

"And then, she closes the boot [trunk], gets in the car, and opens the pocket [ashtray]." Fusena drew a deep breath. "I watch this Accra lady [*sarcasm*] spend plennntttyyy bills inside, with more dey [is] inside. But," Fusena said, her voice beginning to climb, "she digs in the car cup to give me coins!" shouted Fusena, her voice deep with anger. "Hehr!" said Fusena, clapping her hands at the indignity and telling us how she refused to hold out her hand to receive the money.

"And so . . . I start to beg," said Fusena, reenacting how she cast her eyes toward the ground in deference, cupping her hands in a gestural request. "Ma,

Madam, please," repeated Fusena. "The money is small. Add something, please," Fusena retold, now pleading.

Now shouting, Fusena broke the fourth wall of the scene and narrated, "She ons [turns on] the car. Whoosh. The air-con[ditioner] is on. Full blast. I can even feel it as I stand by the door. This fucking lady says to me, 'Please . . .'"

Tani cut in to complete Fusena's sentence. "Please, I don't have change," she mimicked, her voice high and shrill, imitating the feminized demureness of upper-class Ghanaian English, tinged with accents from elsewhere.

"Add something please," pleaded Fusena.

She took a break in the reenactment to make a narrative observation. Balling both her hands into fists, she said, "I tried so hard to refuse the three cedis she's trying to give me," punching the air. Tani leaned back into a relaxed pose, almost lying flat on the sidewalk, looking away. It was hard to tell whether she was really disinterested or frustrated by the series of events being shared. Fusena continued and told us that the Accra lady pretended she didn't hear, pulling her car door shut. She rolled down the window, holding the coins. "Take it," the woman said, repeating, "I don't have change." Fusena stood her ground until the car began to creep in reverse. Fusena knew that once the wheel straightened, her chance to earn any money would be completely lost. Defeated and disgusted, she opened her hand to receive the offered coins.

Fusena started the story sitting atop an upturned carrying pan. Then, she stood in the space between the nook and wall to reenact how she reached out her hand to collect the money. Her voice now dropped to a near whisper, Fusena continued. "You see, you think they will pay you well because they drive big-man cars. But this was very very bad." Tani leaned forward, nodding her head in agreement.

"Here I am, climbing the stairs, coming to this place, taking down my pan," said Fusena, glancing at the basin she had just been sitting on. "I take down this heavy load, and without her help, load the car. I do all. We do all this and after you see them spend so much money. So, I think okay, I think a full, nice amount is coming. But this lady," said Fusena, with contempt in her voice, "we walked aaaaaahhh [a long time] and here it comes. She brings the 'Oh-sorry-I-don't-have-change' story. Nonsense."

Cash is the primary mode of transaction; however, the inability to supply small notes and coins is an ongoing challenge when buying and selling.[13]

Sometimes when buyers present a larger-denomination bill, a cranky seller will refuse to take the money and dismissively say, "I don't have change." What follows is a standoff where both parties wait to see who will relent to take action to find change and complete the sale. Fusena's experience with the Accra lady mirrored this frustrating exchange in relation to her head-loading porterage. In her case, Fusena expressed her exasperation as she threw her hands in the air, sucked her teeth, and exclaimed, "Rubbish."

With her lips pursed and her hands on her hips, Fusena continued.

Overwhelmed, Fusena found herself standing motionless in the parking garage for several minutes. As her anger subsided, she descended the stairs. The gray concrete walls had widely spaced security bars that generated a cooling cross-breeze. Each floor of the storied garage, freshly completed by the start of 2008, had four rows of parking spaces, all brightly outlined in neon yellow. When she reached the ground floor, the first thing Fusena noticed was the three unoccupied stores she saw through the blue reflective glass of the opposite building. Then she saw a spandrel underneath the stairs, situated on the corner opposite to where she stood. The shadowy alcove was easily missed with no active businesses nearby. Fusena said the space caught her attention because the nook did not match the design of the stairs she had just descended, which had a locked door underneath.

Feeling suddenly exhausted, Fusena walked over and crouched inside the area. She noticed how the usual traffic din was reduced to a low hum, muffled by the concrete walls. Grateful for this newfound modicum of seclusion, Fusena sat in the cranny and sobbed. Pointing to where Ajara was currently listening, Fusena said, "It was all right here."

We all sat silently for a few minutes. A car passed by at the far end of the garage toward the exit. "I shock," lamented Fusena. Then, her voice barely above a whisper, she added, "Let me see her again, I go do something," in lingering hurt about being treated so poorly. Ajara pulled Fusena into a hug, and they slowly rocked side to side. A few more minutes of quiet passed until Ajara shifted and stood. She balled up her hands and shifted her body into a boxer's stance, punching right jabs and left uppercuts into the air. After a few air strikes, Ajara clapped her hands and made slapping sounds. We all started laughing, except Fusena. Determined to change her friend's mood, Ajara became more animated in her shadowboxing fight, jumping and slapping her hands against the underside of the stairs. "Hehr! Lady! Add something," shouted Ajara. Fusena fought back a smile. On the cusp of making Fusena laugh, Tani joined in, dramatically rolling on the ground. Moaning "Sorry, wai," in her role as the customer, Tani rolled her body into a ball and extended her hand, offering imaginary money. Beads of sweat formed on Ajara's brow from her fully committed fighting role. Fusena finally laughed in appreciation of their effort; her chortle shifted to a belly laugh, with the sound of giggles rising like bubbles in a fizzy soda. Tani's uncharacteristic high-pitch wail, a remarkable departure from her normal contralto voice, pushed Fusena into the humor of the moment. Ajara ended her boxing performance with peals of laughter. The comedy of the moment was a response to the terrible absurdity of Fusena's experience and a satisfying imaginary of revenge. The whooshing sounds of claps and stomps reverberated against the garage walls and echoed through the stairwell.

After Fusena's discovery of the nook, she and her friends spent several months sleeping and socializing in the space. The space helped all of them save money on the weekly rental fees at Old Fadama. In a short time, the women began to store a few belongings in the space, like their bath sponges and toothbrushes wrapped in a change of clothes. The security agreement was that no one outside of the group of five was allowed to hang out in the space and that at least two people would always take up space in the nook. After an early morning unload at Rawlings Park, Sakina and Amena took regular mid-afternoon naps in the nook. Fusena and Ajara slept in the nook most nights and relieved the space to whoever arrived in the early morning from night-market work.

One evening, Esther and I sat under the stairs making small talk with Amena, Ajara, Sakina, and Fusena. Looking outward to the sidewalk, we cracked jokes about the pedestrians, who, from our seated position behind the half wall, looked like shadowy heads floating down the street. We'd created a game to predict what attire people wore as they walked along, throwing out guesses as we waited for the person to walk by the open entryway to see who won. Sakina was always the most garrulous. She never guessed correctly but kept us laughing with her humorous and detailed estimates about the shoes a person might be wearing. Sakina's "dark sousveillance" (Browne 2015, 77) of looking back and watching people below builds camaraderie for porters to be seen by each other while also being concealed and protected from the hypervisibility they experience through most of their day at the market. If walkers crossed the road onto another street before we could see their full attire, Sakina shifted the detailing to where the person might be coming from or going to, and peppered outlandish claims about who was waiting for them at their destination.

This evening and others like it reminded me of my childhood days spent sitting on the stoop in Philly, where we gathered outside to escape the summer heat and shared stories about the goings on in the neighborhood. The stairway of a not-yet-in-use parking garage is not only a temporal sleeping space and nook for porters but also an example of what J. T. Roane (2023) describes as "dark agoras," the transgressive and interconnected forms of gathering that reconfigure space to more emancipatory actions and strategic reorganization of infrastructure. The nook, the woodpile, and the beach, instead of existing solely as an extension or a proxy of Makola, are temporal spaces where relief from constraint unfolds.

Women who worked midday in the afternoon and were paid up on their rent walked back to Old Fadama or Agbogbloshie together. If sunset got underway and Amena, Ajara, and a few others lingered around Rawlings Park, they lapped Okaishie Market or Tema Station one last time before making their way to the nook. Tani and Amena did not sleep in the spandrel most nights, but if Fusena lit a mosquito coil after a few people showed up, it signaled to whoever was there that they were welcomed to hang out.

One evening, long after a mosquito coil burned and was extinguished, Fusena waxed poetically about the individual choices people make to "make it do." "You know," she said, "everyone does a some thing. One person might go to the station to smoke," said Fusena as she cut her eye at me. She then rolled her torso to the right, looking at Amena expectantly. "And some other person goes to do sex for pay . . ." Her voice trailed off as she looked to Amena, before adding, "or play."

"Ayyy," shrieked Tani, doing a little shimmy and slapping the side of Fusena's skirt. Fusena looked back and between me and Amena, eyebrow raised, before leaning her back against the curb and resting her foot on the crook of a step. With this brief observation, Fusena was outlining a key difference between subtlety and secrecy, and offering an explanation of the berth between confidentiality and shame, without moral judgment of either. Amena and I were both concerned with the other person's perception of our presence in the places we had been seen, but Fusena skillfully deploys a disrespectability politic and humor to challenge the pathological narratives of raped, vulnerable, impregnated and abandoned porters (see Huck 2007, Nafrah 2024, Riise 2016). Fusena's observations also have an affective non-judgment toward different modes of pleasure as well as harm. Everyone in the space enjoyed her teasing us, and Fusena was signaling how, in the end, nobody in that group actually cared about how anyone else spent their time.

Sakina playfully nudged Amena's shoulder and said, "So okay, let's be serious. We get plans." From there, Tani and Fusena initiated a brainstorming session on how to strategize the lineup for an NGO feeding event scheduled for the next day. A few days earlier, Tani had learned about an event from the "boardman in a jacket"[14] who came around to Rawlings Park. The boardman had informed Tani that the event would include *kayayei* registration for an upcoming skill training in jewelry making and possibly sewing. Tani said that the NGO worker was promoting services that she "did not want and did not need" but that "it might be fun, since there was food for free."

Amena was less enthusiastic about the program, adding, "If every time they come, we learn sewing and beading, the sellers will be too many. So then, we go from too many *kayayoo* [sic] to too many sellers, just like the ones who sell on the roadside stalls back home."[15] Tani said that the best that tomorrow's event could offer was a chance for her to "go and enjoy the food," with hopes that they might "also have some music." Amena was not interested in learning jewelry "for the second or third time," but she did know a few people who might be interested and planned to loop them in. For Amena, the focus of that nook conversation was to circumvent "the useless 'improve yourself'" speech and strategically access the services offered.

The women decided Amena and Tani would line up for the program. It was scheduled for two in the afternoon, so they planned to arrive around one thirty, suspecting that the event would not start on time and that, although the event was advertised, most people would just join the queue as they walked by and heard about food. Amena and Tani planned to take turns holding their places in line, which would then allow Fusena and Ajara to work nearby. Meanwhile, Fusena and Ajara would join the line with sachets of water to share with the other women who might be waiting, to preemptively temper annoyances people might have about line cutting. Satisfied with the plan, Tani and Ajara stood to begin the walk to Old Fadama. In the nook, Fusena and Amena tucked in for the night.

The next day, I stopped by the event site, a grassy field near a Presbyterian church on Graphic Road, close to the future home of the not-yet-opened Youth Council Park, to check out the scheduled program. A little after one, nothing much seemed to be happening, except for a tent set up in the middle of the field. A row of taxis was idling nearby, and a few children were playing soccer on the opposite side of the field, their peals of laughter echoing across the dusty pitch. A few minutes later, a bright truck parked at the rear gate of the field. From the passenger side, a lanky man hopped out, dressed in khakis and a crisp button-down dress shirt, sporting an orange-and-yellow safety jacket. I thought to myself, "One of Amena's boardmen," and began to walk toward him. As I approached, he eyed me curiously, giving instructions to the driver and the other passenger about unloading the audiovisual equipment. At the same time, a line of people entered from the rear gate carrying chairs. The doors of the taxis that had been idling swung open, revealing cars full of food. I introduced myself as a researcher who worked with porters and said that I had heard about the event and wanted to learn more. The tall young man, Elias, worked for an organization that had partnered with the church for the day's event. He said that if I was able to hang around and help, I was welcomed to stay.

I was busy unfolding chairs and setting up tables with three other people. More boardmen and boardwomen rushed about, and Elias called for someone to start a queue for porters. At about two thirty, I spotted Amena, Tani, and Fusena in the middle of the line and waved. By three o'clock, everything was set up, and women and girls in the line were admitted to enter the park, each receiving a ticket for the meal.

The event went exactly as Amena and Fusena had foretold. Elias was the field coordinator for the event. He stepped to the podium around three thirty to welcome the sixty or so women and girls to the space, "thankful to God that they had come to seek opportunities to improve their lives," his voice booming with sincerity and enthusiasm. Elias did not address the women directly; instead, they were subjects being refereed to and spoken about to the sponsors of the event. After he acknowledged the generosity of the contributors and donors, Elias listed the order of ceremonies, beginning with his introduction of the district director.

I scanned the crowd for Amena and the rest, but I could not see their faces in the audience; their presence was shrouded in the large group of sixty or so attendees. The event proceeded with high formality and protocol: a note of gratitude from the current speaker for the hard work of the previous speaker, a comment about the plight of porters with a dismal statistic, a series of photos taken of each person as they approached, hands shaken with the person who introduced them, and then more photos that captured the crowd and the speaker during their remarks. The second deputy director followed suit, delivering a few acknowledgments to the corporations that supplied the sewing materials and beads for the training, and then welcomed the caterer to the podium. The second deputy director solicited applause for her, the only woman who was part of the official program besides the recipients standing behind the chairs that were lined up about twenty seats deep and under the canopy. At the end of that speech, the porters, who had now idled for more than two hours, were called to divide into two lines, one line for those who wanted to sign up for the sewing course, another for the jewelry-making classes. The flat atmosphere buzzed when the pastor was called to the front to pray, the most important indication that lunch was about to be served. Some women in the crowd, now formed in a semicircle under the tent, rounding the podium and forming on the field, began moving toward the row of tables with the food.

As the undifferentiated recipients of numerous development programs, Amena, Tani, and their friends had enough experiences at events like this to distill that the program was mostly "something to do," a break from the normal bustle of the day, situated within the repertoire of daily hustles. It was just a few hours after the program's scheduled start time, which meant the event was running right on time in terms of what everyone from the nook expected. Silver pans, resembling the same ones used by women as porters, now sat on the tables, covered in plastic to keep food warm. People handed plates down the line in preparation for the buffet as more women stood behind the tables to dish the meals with big spoons. The spread included rice, meat stew, beans, and pasta. During the registration, the registrar shared voice notes in Hausa, Dagbanli, and Twi with women and girls who had phones, along with the information about upcoming training dates.

The event had gone on well past the time I had planned to spend in town. It was nearly dark, I needed to do my own childcare pickup, neither Esther nor Solomon had come along, nor had I managed to wriggle through the crowd closer to Tani and the rest of her friends during the program. But what struck me before I left was that the program ceremonies took longer than the registration and feeding of the group of women. And that, as I was leaving, Elias was calling out for volunteers to help break down the event and "pack out everything" that was left.

Before I departed, I thanked Elias for permission to attend. He thanked me for helping, and we exchanged contact details. After putting Elias's number in my phone, I wrote a text to my fieldnotes app, "The porters portered the porter event . . . 'for the porters!'"

The next time I saw Amena, Ajara, and Fusena, we were back at the nook, which had become a care infrastructure among this group of friends that, in some ways, fulfilled needs and desires that went beyond the scope of the one-day program we had all attended. The organization successfully achieved its goal of sharing information about skill-building opportunities. Meanwhile, Amena, Fusena, and their friends managed to secure their free meal tickets in between their head-loading work, which provided them with both sustenance and some income. Ajara even joined the crew of loaders responsible for packing up the event's tables and chairs. Last, Amena surprised everyone, including herself, by signing up for the seamstress apprenticeship that was scheduled to start in just a few weeks.

For about six months, the nook reminded me of an old-school hostel, albeit with an even more relaxed approach to duties and responsibilities. Every morning, someone would take the initiative to sweep the space, diligently clearing away the dust from the mosquito coils. Amena, always resourceful, came across a discarded green-and-white plastic kettle with a twisted spout and a missing lid. Without hesitation, she brought it to the makeshift haven and stored it for anyone to use if they needed a quick wash. Pieces of cardboard found life as cushions, providing a bit of comfort against the unforgiving hardness of concrete floors. A few articles of clothing began to accumulate in the corner, often wedged beneath the stair step.

The nook had become a sanctuary, but that peace was abruptly transformed one morning when the calming street noise was shattered by the arrival of a contractor and his crew. The cause of the commotion soon revealed itself—the high-pressure water beam needed to initiate the water-remediation process in the parking garage had arrived. The project was overseen by a friendly but resolute structural engineer named Charles, who introduced himself to Fusena as he made his rounds through the parking deck. He informed her that he was going to be working in the area and that she needed to move away from the space before the work ended.

When Sakina and Amena met up with Fusena later that day, Fusena said she planned to wait the crew out and continue sleeping in the nook. However, that night, the same security guard who had spent most of his nights also asleep in the garage shooed them away. Fusena said that when she and Amena approached the side entrance of the building, the guard met them on the threshold, holding the kettle, a bundle of clothes, and the cardboards pieces. Realizing that they were now evicted from the space, Sakina and Fusena slept on the nearby sidewalk and then spent some time each day watching the construction team work as they eliminated the water damage and mold that had been identified. Except for the notice that Charles had given Fusena, the rest of the construction workers did not engage the porters lingering around, and Fusena and the rest never said anything in return. The remediation work was completed in six days. Afterward, Ajara, Amena, Fusena, and Sakina all returned to either renting space in the kiosks with other porters and migrants at Agbogbloshie and Old Fadama or sleeping outdoors, in groups, at the market.

In the nook under a stairway, a small group of women head porters had generated rebellious possibility through abundance and affection, crafting moments of safety that refused to cede all their power to the material scarcities of the day. In no way does this dismiss or undermine the urgency concerning the violence and vulnerabilities that affect porters, nor do I want to overlook the unknown body burdens that may arise from their rest in a place exposed to the toxicities of mold.[16] Neither too can the events, such as NGO sponsored feeding programs, skill building, or highly publicized health screenings (see *Graphic Online* 2023; GNA 2009; Bayor 2007), fully identify the choreographies of care that makeshift spaces afford women porters. The safety-making that takes place through impermanent sleeping arrangements bolsters women's survivability and complements their care relationships (Wooten 2021). Rather than constructing care as an individualized wellness strategy of consumption, in the nook, porters enliven transitory space and affectively peer educate one another about a range of experiences, from leisure and money-saving schemes to harm-reduction in public space (Arjona 2017). Commensal care, repeating and resharing conflicting stories about market drama, money, and theft—all narrated at the proverbial kitchen table of Black feminist politics—helps restore the parts of women's lives that suffer under the mechanized unhumanness of head-loading work.

The hypervisibility porters experience exists within a broader global entitlement to Black women's bodies and their labor, which functions in tandem with invisibility and devaluation of our work. Black femme sociality traces desire and affection as refusals against scarcities. While enjoying a cool breeze, Kesu and Tani cultivate rebellious possibilities and educational abundance for their children. In the nook, Sakina and others launch successful savings plans and share salient advice about which intercity bus drivers take off-the-books transit fees to deliver packages home. In all these instances, care is not executed as an individualized wellness strategy of consumption but as efforts toward well-being, within temporary impermanent arrangements.

Sylvia Tamale writes that for theorization of sexuality in Africa to move past headlines of despair and the "tired polemics of violence, disease, and reproduction" (2011, 30), we must interrogate not only abuse, violence, and the relentless revenge on African women's bodies but also how intimacies creatively exist, function, and flourish. In many instances, the academic attention to autonomy, independence, and liberation in Africa loiters at the level of the state, leaving accounts of sexuality and pleasure to be reified in gender studies discourse, literary analysis and poetry, or critiques about the limits of respectability politics for women's freedom (Nyanzi 2013). With the counterclaim that habits are shaped by the constructs and discontinuities of home, work, and love, this chapter contributes to the growing body of work about the sexual lives of African people that looks beyond colonial exegesis and the exotic in order to amplify the ordinary as a useful analytic of the paradoxes of service labor economies.

Porters are frequently vilified as characters of an informal or street economy, and blamable victims of legitimated precarity and harm. The nonprofit industrial complex of NGOs that work with porters disagrees, arguing that sex as work lacks pleasure and that drug use has no sociable place in the lives of porters. Often, the vulnerability porters endure is exacerbated by these NGOs, and the health-care providers who lack training on trauma, the emotional and social responses that show up in lived experiences, and the non-normative responses porters have to aid and support that remain overlooked as harmful experiences (Page and Woodland 2023).

Because of the numerous ways in which the market exchanges thrive on extraction and exhaustion, creative performances of livelihood, sex, and sexuality that take place are by no means wholly playful. By *extraction*, I mean how Makola Market and others like it rely on poor women's bodies to facilitate the economic empowerment of the middle-class and urban elite. By *exhaustion*, I mean the depletion of agency and the ability of women to lead lives on their own terms. *Exhaustion* also encompasses the fatigue that arises from having to navigate the constraints of time and money as well as the weariness of immobility despite navigating spaces once envisioned as liberatory for women. This exhaustion also underscores a scholarly weariness among feminist scholars toward the persistent attention to capitalist markets as the epitome of financial freedom for individuals and society, despite the overwhelming evidence to the contrary.

Black feminist anthropology bends the ethnography arc away from precarity and marginalization as the sum of people's identity and experiences. Sitting on sandy sidewalks or rocky stairways as a radical listening praxis is a bedrock for taking note of a constellation of desires, daydreams, and disappointments. Black femme sociality[18] makes space for the untidy sexual and social aspects of porter work and negotiations of intimacy. The Black femme sociality of Esther, Sami, Kesu, and Tani's lives are sensually negotiated and sexually informed. Their sociality assembles the attitudes and experiences of women who love women beyond the boundaries of compulsory heterosexuality. Their relationship to prescribed sexual behaviors challenges patriarchal norms without overt confrontation, with the goal of crafting protection against violence and harm.

The earnings of porter work do not shield girls and women from violence, poverty, or social exclusion. This chapter shows how porters scrutinize the spectrum of these experiences, from dangers to harm, dawning desires, and the occasions to hustle, as well as to gain financial resources otherwise not available to them. Kara Keeling argues that Black femmes "haunt" critical inquiries of race, gender, and sexuality because they are "often invisible (but nonetheless present)" and marked by a "highly contested and contingent mode of existence" (2007, 2). Tani, Barakesu, and Esther haunt queer discourse and intimacy in Africa because they resist reliance on self-named identity categories or coming out as a primary framework to discuss their relationships.[19] As bell hooks put it, "Queer not as being about who you're having sex with (that can be a dimension of it), but queer as being about the self that is at odds with everything around it and has to invent and create and find a space to speak and thrive and to live" (2014, 1:27:40).[20] Popular marriage ideals often conceal love's economic aspects or lead with the presumption that love is a necessary ingredient of a good marriage. Guided by the goal of experiencing greater social cohesion and mobility, Barakesu, Tani, and Esther all live in the interstices of personal identity and outward performance. The economies of marriage also mask in the reification of love, leaving ideologies of affection, when they intersect with money, as less authentic intimacies. I argue that Black femme sociality, as an African and African-descendant formation, is the slippage between interiority and identity, performative deference and defiance.

CHAPTER 5

Milly, Rastabroni, and a Hothead

Tropical fruits have ethereal qualities during their market season. After months of high prices and low availability, avocadoes, watermelons, and mangoes suddenly became as ubiquitous as Afrobeat on the radio. Orange droplets ran down the front of Fusena's yellow shirt while a carmine smear stretched from her right knee to the ankle strap of her Crocs-like shoes. Fusena limped toward the truck-tire-turned-chair, swatting at the leaves of a lone and scrappy palm tree, and then folded herself into the wheel's center hole. Esther and I sat, chatting with a few women who were taking a break from unloading pallets. Pointing to the stains on Fusena's shirt, Esther asked, "Is that blood?"

"Yovulu [watermelon]," replied Fusena. The aqueous nature of watermelon could not have stained Fusena's yellow shirt the bright-orange hue I stared at. However, I did not challenge Fusena's claim. But in the shade of the palm tree we stood under, the splotch bloomed a copper tinge. Fusena looked down, suddenly remembering her hands were covered in dust, and furiously rubbed her palms together. Esther raised her opened sachet of water over Fusena's palms, and Fusena vigorously rubbed them under the makeshift faucet. The dirt crumbs sloughed away into muddy streams that rolled down Fusena's fingers, their steady rivulets matching a sudden onslaught of tears.

Worried that people were looking at her cry, Fusena muttered, "My eyes are sweating," as she looked around and wiped her face. A few other Rawlings Park porters glanced sympathetically from their gathering spot behind a truck, and a woman walked over to hand Fusena a strip of cloth to wipe her tears or dry her hands. Fusena's comment did not divert our attention

from the teary dust track racing down her chin. After the water emptied from
the sachet, another woman wrapped her arms around Fusena, who briefly
hesitated before leaning into the hug.

Fusena had dedicated her morning to unloading a truck filled with watermelons. The fruit had just come into season and inundated the market.
"When I was working at the market yesterday, Abbas told me to come very
early because they needed a lot of us to unload," she said, as she shook her
hands in the air to dry. She shook her head ruefully and added, "I had already borrowed a lot of money the last three days, so I really needed to come
here early."

Fusena went to bed early the night before and then woke up around four
o'clock to make the hour-long walk from the sleep kiosk to Rawlings Park.
In equatorial cities such as Accra, dawn typically occurs just before six o'clock
year-round. Fusena said she had been at Rawlings Park since about five-thirty
that morning. She had no money to buy food for breakfast or water for bathing but reframed these facts as activities that would have "slowed down her
arrival to market," especially because she didn't want to borrow any more
money.

When she arrived at the market, Fusena spotted Abbas assisting a mammy
wagon[1] driver as he slid the watermelon-filled pans between two semis near
the center of the parking lot. For the last ten years, the privately managed
parking lot at Rawlings Park/Square has been run by four or five men who
spend the day expertly directing drivers to the unmarked spaces on the dirt
of the semi-paved lot. Abbas has worked at the lot since the early 2000s. He
became the "top manager" in 2016, after establishing a trust with market reg-
ulars, who willingly relinquish their car keys to Abbas the moment they
enter the parking lot from Pagan Road. Each day, Abbas flawlessly navigates
their vehicles into tight spaces on their behalf. Fusena was surprised to see
fruit coming into Rawlings Park on a mammy wagon at the square and Abbas orchestrating the parking. Besides being banned from importation in the
last sixty years, mammy wagons are rare in the capital, and produce from
the hinterland usually arrived in town at the nearby Agbogbloshie Market.
Waiting for the truck to come to full stop, Fusena suspected that the produce
drop was intentionally off the radar of the Accra Metropolitan Assembly
(AMA) or the produce market, given the mammy wagon's peculiar angle in
the middle of the square, where it seemed to be intentionally hidden from

view. Shrugging off her observation once the truck parked, Fusena joined the other porters lined up to receive instructions from Abbas and the truck driver on where to deliver the loads.

Fusena spent two hours unloading pans of watermelon, walking in a trailing caravan to various drop-off places. Along the way, a few restaurateurs asked where she was taking them and if she knew the prices. One of them was Vita, the owner of the restaurant I frequently sat inside to observe what was going on at the park.

On a given day Abbas skillfully handles luxury vehicles from Alfa Romeos and Range Rovers to Benzes and Beemers. The prestige of these cars and the unspoken trust for their care are momentarily bestowed on Abbas when he slides behind the wheel, parks the vehicle, and then holds onto the keys until the driver returns. In addition to orchestrating the entrance and exit of more than fifty cars, managing the schedules of his fellow attendants, parking "special customers," and ensuring that no cars get hit in this intricate process, Abbas anticipates a driver's return and begins the extraction process so that when the driver arrives at the vehicle, it is in position to immediately and easily exit the park.

Abbas also loves to chat. After Abbas nestled a Mercedes G-Wagon into a spot between two other shiny, expensive cars, he walked toward me, Esther, and Fusena.

"Good morning," he said, looking at Fusena. "Well, good morning, now," he slyly quipped, rubbing his chin in feigned concern, barely holding back a laugh. "This morning, your hothead friend this!"[2] he said, looking at Fusena while he pulled out various sets of expensive car keys from his pocket. As if on cue, Abbas joined us to add context to the story Fusena started telling.

Several feet away, Vita watched us. She stood on the threshold of her restaurant,[3] her eyes narrowed and brows furrowed in annoyance. Peering through the rows of cars that separated us, her stony gaze fixed on our group. Noticing her stares, Abbas picked up the cloth Fusena used to dry her hands and wipe her tears and started waving it like a white flag of surrender. Shouting over the noise, Abbas said, "You see, it no be am [it's not them]!" toward Vita, as if the cloth were proof of something. After handing the cloth back to Fusena, Abbas said, "The Accra lady was looking for her, but don't mind her." Fusena cried harder, her angry sobs now audible above the typical market din. Fusena remained unmoved from the wheel of the tire; she breathed a sigh of relief when Vita walked toward the back of the restaurant and out of street view. "Which Accra lady? Vita?" I asked Abbas, wondering if he meant Vita, since she had been staring so hard.[4]

When the mammy wagon was being emptied a few hours earlier, Vita had called Fusena over to inquire about purchasing some melons from the truck. After passing messages back and forth between the pair about the price, Vita instructed Fusena to unload watermelons into the restaurant's storeroom. Once she finished the subcontracted porterage for Vita, Fusena hurried back to the truck for her payment to not miss the driver before he departed. Fusena and the trucker agreed on the number of trips, but the driver initially wanted to deduct the money for the load to Vita's place. Witnessing the exchange, Abbas scolded the driver for being stingy, and he eventually relented, giving Fusena the rest of her pay (about ten cedis). Afterward, Fusena asked Abbas for a little something for coming to the market so early in the day. As Fusena and Abbas took turns recounting the story, Abbas smiled at Fusena's deduction. "You know, she [Fusena] pressured me small, because she knew the truck was not supposed to be here," said Abbas, chuckling as he confirmed Fusena's earlier observation about this particular truck off-load and the mammy wagon's presence at the market.

Taking the driver's idea about seeking wages from Vita, Fusena walked to the restaurant to ask for money for the watermelon transport to the storeroom. Fusena said Vita agreed to pay her, but not before she questioned whether Fusena had skimmed some of the money for the watermelon sale. Fusena said nothing but was seething. Vita paid her, but Fusena, still angry at the accusation of theft, nudged one of the watermelons with her foot as she walked by the storeroom. Soon after, Fusena heard shouting behind her. Turning around, she saw her neat pyramid of watermelon start spilling out of the storeroom. Vita started yelling. The restaurant manager rushed toward Fusena, shouting for her to stop the watermelons as they fell from the shelf, rolling off each other. Fusena said, "As for me, I stood there. Watching them break open." Half a dozen rolled down the sidewalk. As Fusena watched the manager unsuccessfully stop the rolling watermelons, she started laughing.

"That was the end," remarked Fusena. The other women were furious that she found amusement instead of lending a hand with the scattered produce. Emotions flared, and the situation escalated. Abbas said the manager then charged Fusena, hitting her in the face and arms. Caught off guard, Fusena stumbled over a watermelon while shielding her face and arms from the blows. The melee attracted the attention of bystanders, and a crowd gathered, including Abbas, who had watched the scene unfold from an SUV he had parked nearby. Fusena vividly recalled the intensity of the manager's anger, feeling her nails tighten on her arm, breaking the skin. She wriggled out of the manager's grip and fled, leaving Vita watching on the scene, enraged and embarrassed. She heard furious shouts as she ran from the park, fleeing the market.

Fusena took refuge in the nook. She counted her money and was glad to have enough for the week's rent, the *susu* collector, and maybe one person she owed. When she spotted me and Esther, she had just come back to Rawlings Park to see if things had settled down. As Fusena recounted the chaotic incident to us, her voice carried lingering worry. Abbas mentioned that after Fusena left, Vita was demanding money for her ruined watermelons. Abbas talked to Vita, explaining that the truck driver was a friend, promising to hook her up with more watermelon next time. Abbas proudly said, "Well, I park her Volvo every time she comes, so, you know, she trusts me." Before he returned to work, Abbas shook his head, remarking, "Another wild day with these people." I wasn't sure if he meant Vita, Fusena, or both.

Fusena was exhausted and in pain. Esther and I offered to take Fusena home, suggesting we opt for a *trotro* instead of walking and that we pick up some soap and a few things along the way. Fusena agreed. As she stood from the tire, she said, "It's funny how Madam Vita is cool with Abbas, but not me. She trusts him because he parks her car, but he doesn't even know her name. But me, I've carried for her a few times, but she called me a thief and has no idea what my name is."

The composing and decomposing social apartheids that play out at Makola Market are innumerable, but what unites these threads is a shared expectation, among patrons and sellers, of porters as humble, servile, and visible only when needed. Fusena's break in social code, her laugh and the refusal to move on command, is a rejection of the preternaturally respectful African woman. Fusena's behavior is on the spectrum of what Stella Nyanzi (2020) describes as radical rudeness, and the conflict between Fusena, Vita, and the manager over the boundaries of social deference traces the varieties of these expectations. Deferential respect is aged, classed, and gendered but always expected from poor, young women. The less power a woman has, the less free-dom she has to express displeasure outwardly. Fusena displayed subtle anger with her nudge of a watermelon, stemming from Vita's insinuation of theft. That exchange incited spectacular annoyance and anger. Fusena was expected to remain inconspicuous until needed.

The sensibility of hiding in plain sight showed up even when she was back in the anonymized space between the vehicles at Rawlings Park. And in her retelling of her experience, instead of allowing her tears to flow, Fusena de-clared that her eyes were sweating. This all-too-familiar habit of "mourning in plain sight," the dislocation of feeling while also holding space for pain, is a regular occurrence for Black women (Campt 2019, 85). Fusena was angered by the devaluation of her labor, expressing that something human does re-main and that integrity can still exist even in people's bodies that have been instrumentalized (Sharpe 2014; Tamale 2020). Fusena was frustrated by the shrunken categories she was assigned, and her "sweating eyes" bridged emo-tional hurt with bodily expression, but the clever wordplay did not slow the flow of tears pooled in the dimple of her cheeks or the empathy of the women gathered around to comfort her, considering the overblown reactions to her infinitesimal rebellion.

Walking Fusena Home

We set off slowly because Fusena was walking with a bit of limp, in pain. On our way, we greet Aunty Comfort, a vegetable seller who trades on a rolled-out mat on the sidewalk between stalls. Festus, a pirated-DVD seller, greets me with a booming "Aburokyire sister!"[5] as we move closer to Aunty Com-fort's mat. I owned a portable DVD player that I occasionally brought to the market to watch movies as I waited for people to show up for meetings. Weeks earlier, I had bought several movies from Festus. Since then, no matter how often I saw him, Festus pitched for me to buy from him. A top-shelf sales-person with a smooth sales cadence, Festus greeted me with an energetic handshake and smile. He had a stack of over twenty bi-folded envelopes in his right hand, fanned out like oversized playing cards. With a flourish rem-iniscent of a magician, Festus waved his other hand and announced, "I have the latest." It was an impressive array of DVDs; each disc held anywhere from five to ten movies, organized by a specific theme, much like chapters in a book. Like a skilled three-card monte dealer, Festus stopped me, Esther, and Fusena from getting by with his wide-open arms. Festus deftly selected a Tyler Perry film from the middle of the pile. Pointing to the screenshot of Madea on the back of the glossy envelope, he confidently declared, "Brand new. Just for you."

The movie would not be released stateside for another three months, but Festus already had it in stock. "No, no. I'm good," I said, without sharing that I did not watch Madea movies. Sensing my lost interest, Festus tapped his chest, "Buy something from your brother for your sister." Festus was nearly standing atop Comfort to show me the DVDs, his arms now blocking the space between Comfort and me. Undeterred, Festus playfully fanned me with the swatch of DVDs. One more time, Festus asked, "Maburokyire nua [my foreign sister], buy something. Me pa wo kyεw [please]." Aunty Comfort cut her eye at Festus, her pinched smile matching my annoyance.

We all started paying even less attention to Festus as a soap seller turned the corner toward us with something we did want to buy. I absentmindedly murmured, "Next time, next time," a familiar refrain used to decline making a purchase politely. Turning away, Festus briefly lost his balance, his foot hovering dangerously above Comfort's neat pyramid of tomatoes. Recovering his footing but clearly still frustrated, Festus sucked his teeth and muttered "Coconut!"[6] at me, before turning his attention to other pedestrians. "Humph," responded Aunty Comfort, dismissively waving the back of her hand as if to clear the air for us to continue our walk to residential Agbogbloshie.

In this concluding chapter, I want to utilize Abbas's characterization of Fusena as a "hothead," the reference to Vita as the "Accra lady," and Festus's irritation with me, a "coconut," to describe and discuss the significance of monikers. Nicknames and monikers are standard social conventions among Black people worldwide. Whether rooted in cultural history or anecdotal charm, nicknames are often endearments quite distinct from our government names.[7] They memorialize personality traits or behavioral observation or serve as a vicious crystallization of an experience. Nicknames can also mark rivalries and insider talk. In addition to familial and friend- and foe-bestowed nicknames, in Ghana, there are situations where a person may have an "English" name (sometimes a colonial hangover of respectability politics often used for school registration), a faith-related name (for the masjid, confirmation, or baptism), a name that indicates birth order, ethnicity, or gender, which might also have an added "house" name reserved for close family in a household (Awedoba and Owoahene-Acheampong 2017). They are woven into this chapter because they are analytics of a qualitative interplay between aspiration and anxieties, power and affect.

With singular precision, nicknames and monikers artfully render the social codes of everyday life and the tapestry of identity distinctions. In this chapter, I explore how nicknames tease the subtleties of social location and wield power in interactions. I argue that the knowledges from these tensions, whether playful or painful, reflect the epistemic advantages of African feminisms and Black feminist theories for ethnography to show how information and insights are not born from individuals in isolation but instead result from collaborative and intersubjective encounters.

As Esther, Fusena, and I rode in the *trotro*, Esther and I made small talk about vantage points in the various building-based businesses at Rawlings Park, including Vita's, which has long been a restaurant on the northeast corner of Rawlings Square. The restaurant's enviable location on Pagan Road, its proximity to the taxi station and large, shaded outdoor seating made it a perfect place for an ethnographer. For us, the covered area in the back of the restaurant was a bonus because the shelter offered protection from sudden rain.

The space has been home to four different restaurants over the last fifteen years, each with a rebrand fanfare of new plastic tables and chairs, a fresh coat of paint, and a new signboard.[8] Regardless of the restaurant, the menu remains mostly unchanged, consisting of a selection of warm, starchy bases (rice, yam, or potato), protein, and savory soups. During my earliest days of fieldwork, my time was spent around Deeta's Spot. In 2012, a tilapia griller named Geoffrey masterfully enticed Rastas to the entrance of Ital Foods and Juices with his soya kebabs. By 2016, Vita's was in full swing. For a few months after Vita's place opened, a live band came to play on Friday evenings. Until the band showed up, it was easy to miss that the elevated area at the back of the restaurant was a performance stage because the area had previously been used solely for storage, which was now also the setting for Fusena's disastrous watermelon experience.

Alighting from the minivan, we walked a few long lanes until we reached the kiosk where Fusena stayed. Fusena announced our presence as she stepped into the square room, greeting whoever was inside by raising her voice high above the loud static of the humming radio. Sun crept through the swinging door of the wooden stall, casting a long shadow of bodies onto the floor. The four women inside the kiosk glanced and greeted before returning to their own conversation. Fusena ushered us into the front-left corner, overturned her white pan, then lowered herself onto the floor. She asked us if we wanted water before resting her feet on the flat aluminum bottom of the pan. Lying on her back, she pulled her knees toward her chest to stretch her back and neck. Her flip-flops dangled from her toes before they flopped to the floor.

"I tiya," said Fusena, her voice tinged with relief and exhaustion.

At Fusena's right, a clothesline bisected the twelve-by-twelve-foot space with underwear hung to dry. Behind the line, a photograph was pinned to the wall, fixed on one corner by a staple nail. I took the few steps to go around Fusena, now lying on the linoleum-covered floor, to look more closely at the photograph. Humidity had curled the corner of the picture; the right-bottom side was dotted with mold spores. I instantly recognized Sakina as the subject of the picture. I looked toward Esther, who then followed my gaze to the center-right subject of the image. "Kina?" said Esther, using Sakina's nickname. I raised my eyebrows in affirmation. I asked Fusena, "Is this your friend? Do you know her?" Fusena, barely lifting her head from the yellow-print floor, shook her head no.

In the photo, six women are posed beside a truck plastered with an advertisement for ice cream, and the camera captures them laughing at a friend who photobombs the shot. Sakina is pregnant and wearing a white BVD T-shirt that barely covers the fullness of her belly. I remembered the picture from a series of photographs Barakesu snapped of her friends a few years earlier. I wondered how and why this picture was now hanging in this kiosk.

Seven years had passed since these photographs were taken. I didn't remember whether I had visited this side of Agbogbloshie before or been inside this row of kiosk-home spaces. The wooden sheds become indistinguishable with infrequent visits and look alike after passing three or four lanes. Besides Fusena, I also didn't know any of the women currently living in this shack. Thinking through the same set of questions aloud, Esther asked the other women in the room, "Does anyone know them?" as she pointed to the picture. Esther asked the women in Twi, and blank faces and disinterested gazes were returned. Esther asked again in Dagbanli, then Hausa. She said to me, in English, "They don't know them." Then, a woman in the corner farthest from the clothesline, who had been slowly sifting groundnuts in her pan, looked up and said triumphantly in English, "I know this girl."

"How do you mean?" asked Esther. I looked around the room; no one else appeared interested in the question, but the kiosk was suddenly quiet—the woman motioned for us to sit. Esther and I obliged, lowering ourselves cross-legged on the floor. The other women in the space were listening, even if they were not letting on or fully comprehending the English dialogue. The linoleum was sticky with moisture of humidity and the sweat of labor that permeated the cabin. Outstretched like a starfish, Fusena had drifted to sleep.

The room was sweltering, but a bourgeoning uptick in an airy breeze forecast a rainy season shower. Adjacent to the pan of beans was a frond atop a few pieces of cardboard. The bean sifter's name was Halima. Halima described her family as "poor, but not poor poor" because her mother did not farm directly but was manager at the co-op. The household's recent hard times were the result of her father being injured in a car accident and a subsequent slow recovery. Halima attended a missionary school in the area; her mother paid for her uniform and supplies. Most of the women in the co-op were sending their children to school. At Halima's school, boys outnumbered girls three to one.

Halima's mother worked in a shea butter co-op, but with her dad recuperating, there wasn't enough money for household essentials. The goodwill of neighbors had waned, and traders had stopped extending credit to the household for food. As a solution to their financial woes, a "friend's friend" encouraged Halima to seek work in Accra. This family friend of a friend hyped Halima up with the idea that money would be "easy five hundreds" because of the size and number of markets at Makola. Halima was resistant at first, because "it's the farmers' children who are the ones to kaya," but the hope for "fast money" was irresistible. The friend helped Halima get a sleeping space in the room where we all now sat. Halima borrowed one last time for a bit of start-up money, buying cookies in bulk to sell. She never earned enough to pay for rent and food. Halima also explained how humbled she

Figure 1. Porters at Makola Market with Sakina in white, in the center and facing forward. Photograph by Barakesu.

felt when it was the generosity of those same "farmers' children" whom she felt "above" that kept her fed when her friend declined her repeated phone calls and she had no money to eat. Fusena gave her the advice that her English skills would be welcomed at the shops, so she started loitering around the stores with glass windows and air-conditioning to solicit customers.[9] The approach worked, and Halima works between a bridal shop and a linen supply store for caterers. She was proud to tell us that today she was just sorting groundnuts to help the other women in the kiosk. As she sifted through handfuls of shells, Halima leaned forward conspiratorially and said, "Look," drawing out the word for greater effect, "I hear this girl made plenty money doing kaya in Accra." She gestured toward the picture of Sakina and her friends. After blowing peanut skins from her hands, Halima wiped her hands on the apron tied around her waist before she continued.

"I hear that girl made five hundred cedis . . . a day . . . *and* she didn't do sex, sell pills, or anything . . . five hundred cedis a . . . day . . . just kayayoo.

She be haarrd gyal." Esther and I quietly glanced at each other. Catching our unbelieving looks, Halima emphatically added, "It's possible." Shifting from English to Dagbanli, Halima spoke to two other women in the room, motioning to the photo. They nodded and said, "Milly." Esther turned to me and said, in English, a confirmation of Halima's assertions about Sakina, "They call her Five Milly."[10]

It wasn't clear whether the moniker was for Sakina individually or a nickname for the group, but all the women agreed that Sakina and her friends earned five million cedis, moved back "to the north," opened shops, and "hired workers to farm." Halima clapped her hands in agreement, stirring Fusena, who awakened from her nap.

Each woman in the room now debated their proximate relationship to the women in the photograph. Halima said Five Milly was renting in the kiosk just before her arrival. Another woman pointed toward the photobombing figure in the shot and said, "This one took her five million and just enjoying life." Someone else mentioned having a cousin who is friends with the girl on the right and has "seen them around."

Halima's effusive Five Milly commentary is an imaginative rebound within an inescapable daily struggle. Five Milly, as a tale, pools toward an anthropological cornerstone about myths and the seduction they hold in understanding relationships, agency, power, dominance, and oppression (Shulist and Mulla 2022). As a moniker, Five Milly earmarks emotive qualities and elicits indexical responses. This social fact does not detract from or diminish Five Milly as a sustaining archetype to Halima's energetic imaginary, despite each day's income deficit for her and every other porter in the room. It is also a placeholder for the manifest of upward mobility. As a material artifact, the photograph signifies a potential future selfhood that visually imagines Halima's expectations but wildly overestimates what five hundred cedis can accomplish. The wage myth conflates the personal and the communal to bring dreaming into the common threads of experience, with the image a placeholder for futurity. The object of Halima's gaze is Sakina and her friends, a moniker attached to the collective, who are individually unnamed. "Five Milly" is incommensurable with the material conditions and ideological frameworks that structure porters' lives in Accra. The conversation and the photographs are a resignation and rearticulation of the way bodies are reified for labor and fetishized through gazing and consuming. The picture then serves as a trickster image, unattached to the person Esther and I know, but saying a lot about future fantasies.

The sorting complete, Halima stood to scoop beans into plastic sleeves in preparation for sale. She took the pile of split beans and poured them into a can. The metal can held the beans Halima allocated for herself. When dried brown beans split open and expose the white pulp, they are less attractive to customers, driving down the price of the sleeve of beans. The repurposed tomato tin that now stored her portion overflowed with whole and split beans. This is a concession Halima affords herself for the tedious work. From the sort piles there was also a mound of pebbles Halima plucked from the pan. She walked to the threshold and threw them outside.

Still sitting on the floor with Halima, Esther and I leaned across our cross-legged knees to confer with each other.

"Should we tell her?" whispered Esther, leaning in.

"Which part?" I asked, answering Esther's question with a question. Uncertainty clouded my response as I wondered what "tell" Esther was referring to—the fact that we knew Sakina, that Five Milly/Sakina lived just about thirty minutes' walk from where we currently sat, or that Five Milly, as a story, had a few missing subplots? For instance, the child Sakina was pregnant with in the photo was now a five-year-old registered at school in the nearby Mamprobi neighborhood. Sakina did return to her hometown, pregnant, and returned to Accra after the baby was born. But also, Sakina sends remittances to her husband from the money her boyfriend makes selling imported apples. As far as I know, Sakina had no plans to return to her hometown.

With these thoughts racing in both our minds, Esther and I remained quiet. Instead of continuing our wordless conversation over intense eye contact, I reached in my bag and grabbed my phone. I scrolled through the photo gallery until I found my picture of Sakina that matches the one hanging on the wall. In my version of the photograph, Sakina is noticeably more pregnant, her bodied angled away from the camera lens, which provides a clearer view of her belly peeking beneath the white T-shirt she is wearing. I then held the phone out.

"Ayyyyy," shrieked Halima, grabbing the phone, snapping her fingers in delight. Fusena stirred briefly before returning to her nap.

"Five Milly" is an informative invention of the ways in which habits can assemble sensibilities around care and reciprocity. For Halima and the women in the kiosk, Five Milly preserves agency amid pervasive fore-closures on financial freedom (Manful 2022). This perspective highlights how daydreaming and imagination hold significance for individuals who lack resources. Five Milly, as a moniker, is a cognitive and emotional re-source that, in the absence of material wealth, holds space for imaginative thinking and a means of hope and promise. Five Milly carves out space for Halima to think beyond her immediate circumstances and envision alternative outcomes for the present. Generatively, then, Five Milly is more than a resilience exercise but a site for creative problem-solving and self-possession.

The spatial displacement of poor, mostly Black and Brown people and the regularization of their death, disposability, and surveillance are unfortunately not exceptional. However, to homogenize Africa as a naturalized site for these conditions is also a disservice to the intellectual endeavors of anthropology and Black studies. The North Atlantic hegemony in Black feminisms engen-ders the systemic exclusion of Afro-feminisms and African feminist theories and methods in ethnography (Blay 2008). These omissions, combined with the androcentrism of African ethnography and an overly determined per-spective of African women's bodies as the vessels of tradition or submission, contribute to the frequent absence of African women's interior lives in eth-nography. I believe that ethnography grounded in the theories and methods of African feminisms reveals how the global economy exploits all margins to drive capital accumulation and dispossession.

In the preceding chapters, I orient Makola Market and the porters who work there as part of a larger tapestry of development after colonialism, as informed by antiblackness and the aspirations of modernity.[11] Still, I have avoided engaging Makola Market as a metaphor for the market economy, even as anxieties about development, housing, living wages, and tourism are convergent and widespread. But what that space does lend itself to is the importance of the capital city as an instructive site for urban ethnography of Africa. It is also with intention that I have not parsed the blurred bound-aries of head-loading as work or labor, because each of these concepts yields the dizzying dosages of anxiety, violence, and harm that women experi-ence, as well as inciting autonomous acts, substantive creativities, and care-fully orchestrated intimacies. I do accomplish this task only partially,

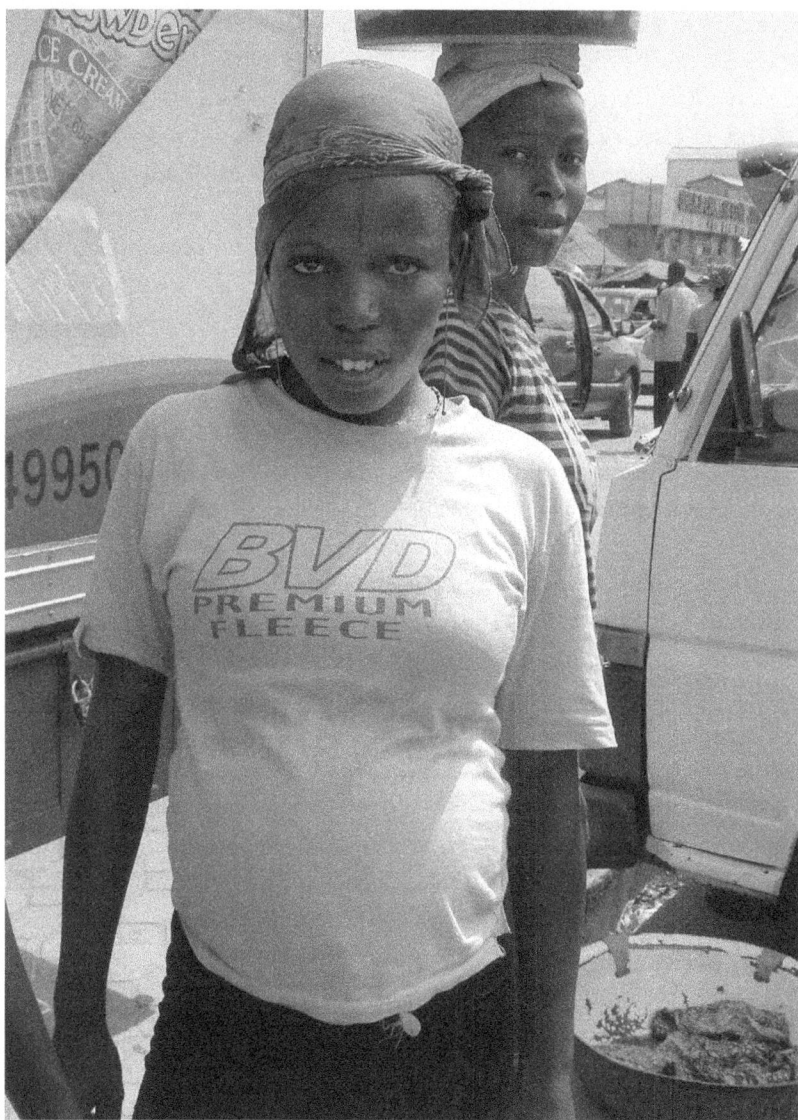

Figure 2. Sakina. Photograph by the author.

because the issues I attend to have and have had numerous entry points. There are other people who could have been part of this project, including male truck pushers, additional transportation operators, and more market traders, to also see how gender, race, and sensibilities of modernity come into being. However, I chose women who work as head-loaders in Accra's Makola Market because of my political commitment to show how race, sexuality, class, and gender matter in the lives of African women when thinking about modernity and mobility in Africa. One of the major points this book has made is that the distance is short between blackness as a global intellectual conversation and the enactment of social exclusion and modernity in Ghana. Class position, gender, and geographic locale are determinants of privilege that supposedly sidestep race and ethnicity in Ghana. But, as I have argued, investigating women's experiences as head-loaders in Accra demonstrates how racialization of blackness, with origins in colonialism and slavery, extends into contemporary modes of capital accumulation. Living with economic and material downward mobility influences how women domestic migrants experience Accra and negotiate relationships. Simultaneously, whether they are viewed as an impediment to the vision of return offered by the state to the diaspora or publicly scolded for taking up too much space while they work, women head porters, like many laborers in Ghana, are excoriated in dreamscapes of modernity. I use interviews and stories to shed light on the way that ideologies of race, sexuality, and feminized labor are mirrored in the day-to-day interactions in the city. I argue that forms of modernity making occur through antiblackness and show how Africa is not immune to these processes. The various chapters of this book reveal how these structures of social (im)mobility map onto the lives of women head porters.

Through their reconfiguration of feminized household labor in the last thirty years, girls and women are part of the hypervisible and embodied undercarriage of modern Accra. Head-loaders, a pioneer generation of gig economy workers, are the proto-cyborgs of Accra's trader and human transport sectors. A large body of infrastructure scholarship often focuses on the built environment and projects such as rail lines, sewage systems, and power plants. In Black and Indigenous geographies, infrastructure regularly includes attention to the relationality and ecological interdependencies of physical spaces. The subsequent ordering of processes and social interactions (Star 1999), coupled with the pandering to diasporic returnees for the economic development plans of the city, accelerates the dispossession of various inhabitants in the city. And porters and other laborers who are considered strangers bear the heaviest burdens. Porters' bodies carry forward a posthuman imaginary in a body that is considered a barrier to modernity. Cyborgs are the hybrid of machine and organism, a posthuman perspective where very little differentiates bodies from technology. The irony that porters do not rely on digital media or wearable technology to complete their work does not preclude them from being as smart, adaptable, or innovative as other technologies. Rather than argue the validity of head-loading as gig work, *Headstrong* shows how place, race, gender, and sexuality unfurl in an African city and underscores the centrality and vitality of African feminisms and Black feminist ethnography for illuminating these complexities. Head porterage is a sentient praxis, a sociopolitical experience, and shows how blackness is negotiated and navigated in racially homogeneous places. In addition, the book examines how the somatic infrastructural legacies of slavery and colonialism show up in work relationships and class dynamics. Ultimately, I analyze ordinary commentaries about the surveillance and scrutiny of marginalized bodies—framed as safety measures to sanitize sidewalk and transportation areas—in efforts to make sense of the increasing vilification of street hawking and loitering to shed light on public interpretations of modernity.

Headstrong is a Black feminist orientation toward unexceptional, often unnamed, women. The book examines how women's "presencing" represents the efforts porters make to surpass the prescriptive categories associated with the working poor (Awachie 2020). The book takes seriously the imaginaries and emphatic conversations of women laborers as the central analytic in order to align ethnography with headstrong people. Women's efforts, whether physical acts or emotional labor, anchor spatial knowledges about how markets are experienced, understood, remembered, and talked about. Moreover, the use of radical listening as a method and a citational praxis of African and African-descendant feminism expands femme sociality as a sexual politics, highlights blackness as a somatic and expressive affect of modernity and illustrates class as a metonym of race. Modernity as an affective project explains how blackness reproduces exclusion in Ghana for residents outside the dividends of social mobility.

This book also unpacks why there are no shortcuts to understanding the interiority of people's lives, especially when we do not share competencies in each other's languages or clearly marked common ground. Porters and their lives as well as my personal commitments and professional relationships with them often exceeded the social and political constructs mapped onto our bodies. I also believe the ideological and methodological challenges of ethnographic research are further complicated by the racial politics of scholars who work at the intersection of African studies and Black studies. My hope is that my use of African and African-descendant feminist frameworks brings African anthropology into closer conversation with Black studies in a way that showcases the capaciousness of this scholarship to chart less oppressive futures and, hopefully, less extractive ethnography. Intellectual autonomy, guided by an ethic of care, is the key to survival, not only for our interlocutors but also for any academic commitment to antihegemonic intents and outcomes.

To be a daughter of the diaspora who criticizes state and social practices of a nation-state regularly idealized as a beacon for the diaspora is perhaps to court criticism. I hope that being a Black feminist scholar from the Global North writing *Headstrong* is not a foray into the diaspora wars but is seen as an effort to name and analyze how the tentacles of global white supremacy exist alongside filial blackness. The book, in essence, is about relationships that are forged and endured in the crucible of struggle and focuses on the ordinary to take account of the sustaining qualities of social conflict as well as intimacy. For the women in this book, porter work is, in part, an attempt to push against the systemic downward mobility of agriculturalism and global capitalism. In thinking about those efforts, the book reckons with the limits of ethnography to valorize autonomy amid the crushing weights of social exclusion, antiblackness, cisheteropatriarchy, inadequate housing, and material dispossession. My aim with *Headstrong* is twofold: to challenge the narrative investment in women's bodies as sentient representations of a fledgling modernity and to explore the particularities of precarity for women and girls who porter. I prioritize the creative expressions of home, households, and love to understand how social networks sustain the aspirational futures that porters envision. Porters live in the pathway of habituated harm, but there are assuagements that run parallel with their struggles. However, as attentive as *Headstrong* strives to be, ethnography cannot dismantle the inequities that organize porters' lives or alter the logics that structure the marginalization porters endure. That project demands continued consciousness-raising, collective mobilizations, and movement building to dismantle oppression and cultivate sustainable livelihoods.

NOTES

Introduction

1. *Kayayoo* (sing.), female head porter; *kayaye/kayayei* (pl.).

2. *Chronotope* was conceptualized by Mikhail Bakhtin (1984) to describe the interconnectedness of time and space in literature. I draw on Paul Gilroy's (1993) expanded discussion of *chronotope* as the flexible and contingent characteristics of belonging that relate to race, mobility, and globalization.

3. In 2015, Esenam Nyador was initially refused membership to several taxi unions because of her gender (Benke 2016).

4. The perception of porters as "low-skilled workers" is in tandem with the millions of workers worldwide who are minoritized and/or immigrants in the West. This perception situates day laborers as a social problem rather than as surplus workers in who live in response to the employment sectors that structure the conditions of their work. In the West, the low-skill narrative is regularly attached to immigrants who do not speak the dominant language of a place, which speaks more to the language hegemonies of places than it does to intellectual capacity.

5. Created in 2001, the Ministry of Women and Children's Affairs (MWCA) was renamed the Minstry of Gender, Children and Social Protection (MGCSP).

6. Pat Robinson et al. ([1970] 2005) explored how Black women in Africa and the diaspora have been represented through overlapping discourses of dehumanization and mechanization that deny Black women the opportunity to feel and express a full range of emotions. These animalistic and mechanistic frameworks then serve the broader stereotype of the tireless Black superwoman (Wallace [1987] 1990). In *Black Sexual Politics* (2004), Patricia Hill Collins analyzes how the dichotomous stereotype of the strong Black woman and the weak Black man denaturalizes Black people to sustain overarching ideologies of Black bodies functioning in the service of white supremacy and capitalist accumulation.

7. Compulsory monogamy is the idealization of monogamous relationships as the normative composition for romantic partnerships, particularly those that include marriage. As coercive social mandate, compulsory monogamy induces pressure and stigma against people who choose nonmonogamous relationships (Moultrie 2018).

8. The prevalence of homosociality as an acknowledgment of the emotional closeness between men is also a scholarly effort to affirm male relationships while avoiding the toxicities of masculinity as well as accusations of being gay.

Chapter 1

1. I did not have the opportunity to speak directly with most porters about the 2021 fire, which occurred at the height of the COVID-19 global pandemic, when travel restrictions were

still widely in place. Also, most do not privately own mobile phones. Porters who do have access to cell phones do not carry them around at the market when they are working.

2. Ministry of Employment and Labour Relations in Ghana, 2022, https://www.melr.gov.gh.

3. For instance, up until British annexation in the early twentieth century, Hausa and Mande people controlled and managed much of trans-Saharan and regional trade in northern Ghana (Awedoba 2006).

4. During fieldwork in 2017, a friend asked me to bring step pedometers for their walking group. I bought six, but only three were needed by the time I arrived in Accra. When I was talking with Zaynab about the remaining three, she asked about whether I had ever walked the whole day alongside women as they carried. I had not. Most of the time I spent with porters was between jobs, over a meal, or in the evening, when they were not working. She suggested I give the pedometers to them; they would make good gifts, especially because the devices had additional features like alarm clocks and thermometers, and they would give me a better sense of how much walking women do daily. Taking Zaynab up on this fabulous suggestion, I gifted the pedometers to three women and asked them to share them with a friend for the next three weeks and record their steps for three of their workdays. I asked that at least one of the records be from Tuesday, Friday, or Saturday, the busier market days. Altogether, the group recorded fifteen daily readings. The median reading was 14,218 steps a day. The average steps per day was 13,789. None of these values includes the steps that are part of the daily commute.

5. *Chale wote* are open-toed footwear, often referred to as bedroom slippers or flip-flops outside of Ghana. The Ghanaian pidgin English phrase means "friend, let's go," suggesting the ease and convenience of sliding the shoes on and heading out. *Chale wote* are typically made of rubber or other lightweight materials, making them practical for everyday wear in warm climates. *Chale wote* also carry significant class and social markers: on the one hand, one can easily be denied entry into nightclubs and restaurants if wearing rubber *chale wote*; on the other hand, Ghanaian royalty and traditional leaders wear adorned and embellished leather *chale wote* as part of their traditional regalia.

Chapter 2

1. Christina Sharpe (2012) describes the hyphen as an "irresolvable distinction" from the holistic viciousness of antiblackness. Davis (2024) suggests how the hyphen refuses the overdeterminism of language and does not "foreclose other openings." In this chapter, I consider that insight as a framework for consideration of *-ness* as a contribution to that conversation. As a holder for the affectual, embodied, and expressive qualities of harm and hurt, I use *antiblackness* in order to call attention to the way porters make sense of and manage their experiences with racism and the sociohistorical structures that engender those burdens. Following Annie Olaloku-Teriba's (2018) instructive essay on the historical logics of antiblackness in Africa, and the ahistorical theorizations of antiblackness that exclude African experiences, I chart antiblackness as a set of historically situated sensibilities that are somatic, informed by bodily knowledge, and sometimes without spoken articulations or utterances.

2. *Drylongso*, the title of John Langston Gwaltney's 1980 book as well as a Black American idiom, is a colloquial expression that describes the attitudes and perspectives of the ordinary, working-class Black people living through multigenerational subordination in society. In a similar vein, this chapter theorizes modernity from the perspectives of working-class and poor Ghanaians to show how belonging in a contemporary society is understood, experienced, and explained.

3. As of 2018, there were sixteen administrative regions of the country. Before then, there were ten regions, with the Northern Region, just south of Burkina Faso and about five hundred miles from Accra, being the largest of these.

4. There are over sixty ethnic groups and three hundred different languages spoken in Ghana, so here I am not suggesting that race replace ethnicity as an identifier in Ghana. However, the interplay between ethnicity and race warrants consideration within the global politics of blackness.

5. The imposition of colonial tribal designations did not reflect the complex precolonial conduits of power that overlapped negotiations about protection, taxes, tributes, land access, and slavery. Benjamin Talton (2010) explains how Rattray expressed aversion to the colonial preference for "tribes" as the primary framework for understanding political structure and social organization in Ghana.

6. See Josephine Beoku-Betts's (2005) incisive overview of the representations of African women in academic discourse from the nineteenth and early twentieth century for a more scholarly treatment of these themes.

7. Following a 2022 trademark-infringement lawsuit filed by the California-based festival company Coachella, Afrochella was renamed AfroFuture.

8. This gesture toward an invitation to repatriate is fraught with economic expectations and implications. In 2000, Ghana instituted the "Right of Abode" law, which allowed "any person of African descent" to apply for residency and citizenship in Ghana. However, eligibility for Right of Abode is predicated on applicants' ability to make a "substantial contribution to the development of Ghana," which is subject to review by Ghana Immigration Services (Asare 2019).

9. Mami Wata ("mother of water" in Ghanaian pidgin) is a transnational water deity of Africa and the diaspora. Often visually depicted as a mermaid or a woman in water, Mami Wata bestows economic prosperity and fertility on those who honor or worship her. One of the most recognizable Africana deities, she is regularly cast as the "fallen angel" in Pentecostal proselytizing (Meyer 2008, 389). Mami Wata's beauty and seductive qualities are also metaphorized in the strong current and ocean tides that can sweep a person away. The rejection of Mami Wata and her powers is viewed as a testimony of Christian faithfulness, signals one's "complete break" from local traditions, and captures the "ambivalent views about modern life" among Accra residents (Meyer 1998). Still, these shifting beliefs about Mami Wata do not completely diminish the deference and respect Ghanaians have for the strength of ocean water or fears of drowning from the strong current and undertow of the Atlantic.

10. Osei Alleyne (2017) charts a social history and popularity of reggae and dancehall music in Ghana that explores how Rastafarianism fosters diasporic kinship in Accra.

11. Also called brukina or burkina, in reference to the drink's Burkina Faso origin story, dege has risen in popularity in Accra since 2015. Still, the drink is considered a "northern drink," especially because millet is primarily grown in the savanna of the country.

Chapter 3

1. Photography has long been part of a toolkit of methodologies used by anthropologists. In early anthropological fieldwork, photographs served as an evidentiary tool for researchers to recall events. In more contemporary usage, photographs served as an elicitation technique, where researchers used their photographs to access and collect stories from community members (Harper 1987). Photovoice is a participatory method, defined as a way for people to "identify, represent, and enhance their community through a specific photographic technique" (Wang and Burris, 1997, 369) that allows participants to pose meaningful questions and reflect on their community. Increasingly common as a feminist activist research method in feminist ethnography,

photovoice can foster critical dialogue and facilitated group discussions among participants (Davis and Craven 2016). Celebrated for its participatory aspects, photovoice is also cautioned for its potential to reimagine positivism in ways that center aesthetics and notions of authenticity in research findings (Shankar 2016).

2. Also called *adisaa* in Twi, *alasa* is a seasonal yellow-orange oval-shaped fruit that is sour and has a consistency like chewing gum. *Yooyi/yoyi* (also called a velvet tamarind) is an edible fruit soaked in water and made into a drink.

3. At the time of this encounter, the global ride-sharing services Bolt and Uber were not operational in Ghana. Their services were introduced in 2016. *Dropping* is a term that describes hailing a taxi from the ride side and negotiating with the driver to price a destination. Although the smartphone-based rideshare services are extremely popular in Accra, dropping is still widely used. Margaret Grieco et al. explore the gendered dynamics of formal and informal transportation economies in Accra (Grieco, Apt, and Turner 1996); see also Robert Ohene-Bonsu Simmons's (2018) analysis of how digital technologies disrupt the private taxi industry, which is where dropping is most common.

4. As discussed in Chapter 1, *chale wote* is a Ghanaian pidgin English term for flip-flops, usually associated with the shibboleth "*chale*, let's go." There are competing arguments about the genealogy of the colloquial word *charlie/charle/chale/chaley*. The highly expressive and multifunctional term's meaning depends on context, locale, age, gender, and intonation. For example, Joseph Benjamin Archibald Afful (2006) describes it as a term used between strangers as well as friends to build camaraderie. Kari Dako (2002) explains that it means "friend," "dude," or "buddy." The origin of the term is unclear, but it has been described in association with Charlie or Jack, the commonplace namesakes of British colonials, or as a Krio expression that arrived with repatriated previously enslaved people resettled in Sierra Leone and Liberia (Asuro 2015).

5. In Black feminist thought, care has always been centered as radical relationality or practices of habit and doing that considers well-being as liberatory acts and a means of survival (McClaurin 2001). Care is an effort to choose emotional and physical wholeness, which is an act of defiance in an oppressive world.

6. Maurice Merleau-Ponty (2011) is a foundational scholar of phenomenology and the philosophy of the self and the body, but he does not address the intersecting particularities of bodies and their politics of race, class, gender, sexuality, ability, and so on. Black and Brown feminists have the lion's share of that work, to assert lived experience as a site of transformation and use visual methods in that capacity (see Bunster B. 1977; Bowles 2016; Campt 2017; Shobat and Landry 2018).

7. Moya Bailey coined the term *misogynoir* to classify anti-Black and misogynistic representation of Black women in visual cultural, including photographs and digital spaces. In *Misogynoir Transformed: Black Women's Digital Resistance* (2021), Bailey uses the framework to detail how digital spaces are deployed to refuse misogynoir and create online communities of resistance and transformation.

8. Catherine E. McKinley's *The African Lookbook* (2021) elegantly explores femininity and subjectivity alongside the social lives of cloth, print, and photographic styling and the circulation of those images over a hundred-year period. In the book, McKinley argues that although women are conceived as subjects to the colonial gaze in images, photographs are also powerful counternarratives to the poverty pornography of global media images. Prasse-Freeman (2020) makes a similar argument about refusal as the pre-emptive denial of claims to access, which is similar to the tactics Rahida deployed in rejecting participation in the photovoice project.

9. Cooktops, stovetops, and ovens are more widespread in middle- and upper-class households. Gas tanks are expensive and can be cumbersome to fill and refill. Even in those homes, a coal pot is sometimes preferred, and used outdoors, when someone wants to keep the aroma of food from inside the house.

10. *Hajia* is a common honorific used toward Muslim women, irrespective of whether they have completed hajj, or pilgrimage to Mecca.

11. In the Hausa language, *shinkafa* means "rice" and described a variety of rice-based dishes. In the Twi language, the *ky* spelling confers the *sh/ch* sound. Described as *kyinkaafa* or *shinkafa* in Accra, in Kumasi, the dish is called *kwenkwen*.

12. The area from the eastern edges of Korle Lagoon holds one of the largest e-waste dumping sites in West Africa (Little 2021). In the popular media, the entire area, ranging from the lagoon to Agbobloshie Market has problematically been nicknamed Sodom and Gomorrah, after the twin cities destroyed by God (Ogbamey 2002).

13. Polytank, whose tanks are made from polyethylene, is the most popular water-storage-container brand in Ghana. Akin to the way *Hoover* stands in for *vacuum cleaner* or *Xerox* describes a multifunction copier or printer, irrespective of the manufacturer, water tanks are called *polytanks* or *polys*. The inequitable access to networked infrastructure around water supply led to the widespread popularity of water tanks. As a response to a highly variegated water infrastructure, polys are used to maintain a consistent water supply. In the settlements near Makola, porters purchase water from vendors for their daily needs. Water that is for immediate use is usually carried in pans. Yellow plastic containers are used for longer storage. Those yellow containers are called "Kufuor gallons" (after former president John Agyekum Kufuor). During the Kufuor administration, there was a nationwide water shortage, and Ghanaians stood in line for hours with the yellow gallons to purchase water (Adom 2016).

14. Andrew S. Harvey and Maria Elena Taylor (2000) describe "time overhead" as the minimum number of hours a household uses to address the basic chores necessary to maintain the care of its members. This includes the time spent preparing meals, cleaning, collecting water, washing clothes, and gathering the materials necessary to complete these tasks. They argue that households with lower time overhead, which depends on the number of adults and children in a household and their abilities to support various tasks, have a higher capacity for well-being.

15. Amena and Balima never referred to Accra as their home, only their natal communities. This is why I use Whitney Battle-Baptiste's (2010) conceptualization of "homeplace" to describe the container and other living quarters as landscapes that do provide moments of relief. Although Battle-Baptiste's reference is related to the archaeology of captive African communities on plantations in the United States, *homeplace* stands in as a useful contrast to *home*. The distinction women make about Accra, as not home, opposes southern Ghanaian sentiments of the capital city as an always-desired destination for migrants.

16. A fine-toothed comb with a long, skinny handle ("like a rat's tail") used to divide hair into symmetrical parts on the scalp.

17. The issue of hair straightening and beauty standards commingle with the racialization of aesthetics (Caldwell 2003; Wingfield 2008; Thompson 2009). In conversations in other contexts, women were more attached to a class sensibility that straight hair confers rather than a racialized one, as well as adulthood rather than a consciousness around "good" or "bad" hair. In many public-school settings throughout the country, all students are required to wear their hair short and cropped. The permission to grow one's hair out is available to girls toward the end of high school. The sense of attractiveness porters connect to hair is more about the performance of adulthood and autonomy than an adherence to "Western" beauty standards assigned to Black women who straighten their hair.

18. Of Yoruba origin, *esusu* (rotating credit) is a savings system used across West Africa (Imam and Tamimu 2015). In Ghana, agents called *susu* collectors travel through the market or operate stands to collect a fixed payment amount of daily contributions from their customers. The amounts are recorded in a savings ledger. After an agreed-upon period (usually thirty days), the funding is returned to the customer, and the *susu* agent keeps the first day's contribution as

a service fee. This savings strategy helps minimize risk against theft, but the practice is not state-regulated.

19. Here I use Savannah Shange's (2019) articulation of "Black girl ordinary" as a strategy of persistence within the afterlives of slavery in conversation with Aimee Meredith Cox's (2015) choreographies of citizenship as a method Black girls deploy to speak back and engage with the state.

20. As I mentioned earlier in the book, in anthropological studies, African women are often talked *about* as subjects with less consideration for the interiority of African women's lives. In *The Sovereignty of Quiet: Beyond Resistance in Black Culture*, Kevin Quashie (2012) describes "quiet" as an expressiveness of inner thoughts that informs outward expression. Similarly, Nyaradzayi Gumbonzvanda, Farirai Gumbonzvanda, and RochelleAnn Burgess (2021) question why the emotions and imaginaries of quiet activism are devalued as part of women's health by organizers in Zimbabwe. They argue that because women's resistance is neither silent nor boisterous, their collaborative and insurgent habits are overlooked.

Chapter 4

1. "Black nonchalance," the practices and habits that express "a kind of *non-feeling*, an *undoing*, a *non-knowledge*, a refusal to know that isn't rebellious or ignorant but above concern" (Serpell 2020, 47), is not necessarily resistance or even refusal but a repertoire of performances and emotional sensibilities of betweenness that are expressed amid the minefields of racism, poverty, harm, and violence Black people endure in daily life (Serpell 2020).

2. Barakesu does not know her exact age but estimates she was between about eleven and thirteen years old when she and Daáre were betrothed. A few years older than her, Daáre left home just before high school to work on a cocoa plantation near the Ghana-Togo border. Betrothals are followed by long engagements, until each person is considered financially and socially prepared for marriage. Little to no stigma is attached to the sexual relationships between people who are engaged, as a forthcoming marriage is expected.

3. For Tani and Barakesu, polygamy is a fabulous beard. In queer colloquialisms, *beard* usually refers to a person who knowingly or unknowingly acts as a romantic partner or date in order to conceal a person's not-straight sexual orientation. In this example, I invert the term *beard* and claim polygamy as a concealment of queer relationships.

4. Polygamy has been widely covered across the humanities and social sciences with an array of work that has examined how polygamy is tied to essentialist notions of kinship (Lewis 2011) and is a discursive manifest of cisheteropatriarchy (Bowan 2013) and a facade for Islamophobia and Afrophobia (Gilliam 1998).

5. AbdouMaliq Simone (2004) introduces the idea of viewing people as a form of infrastructure. Simone suggests that the interplay between various social groups and the economic collaboration between individuals living at the margins of urban life, who are crucial to the city's operations, contribute to the perceived worth of a city, much like how transportation and utilities are typically regarded as indispensable components of a functional infrastructure.

6. In the United States, *beard* and *lavender dating* are colloquial expressions that describe a relationship created to conceal a person's or couple's sexual identity or divert attention away from their non-cis-hetero or nonnormative dating practices or sexual habits.

7. "Bey, you know" is a rhetorical expression that signals mutual agreement between people about the current conversation.

8. In *Knowing Women: Same-Sex Intimacy, Gender, and Identity in Postcolonial Ghana*, Serena Owusua Dankwa (2021) explains how, during her fieldwork, Ghanaian women rarely elaborated on their same-sex relationships during life-history accounts or structured interviews.

Narratives about same-gender sexual intimacies are usually part of a larger retelling of events, partially because of stigma attached to same-sex relationships and because conversation about sexual intimacies rarely occurs between people who do not have preexistent close ties.

9. This conversation took place years before the 2021 introduction of the "anti-gay bill," but its looming parliamentary passage heavily influences the writing choices of this section. Same-sex relationships are already criminalized as the result of the British colonial penal code, Offences Against the Person Act of 1861, and Section 104(1)(b) of the Ghanaian Criminal Offences Act 1960 (Act 29; Diwakar 2021). The popularly described "anti-gay bill," formally known as the Promotion of Proper Human Sexual Rights and Ghanaian Family Values Bill, includes a litany of virulent anti-queer provisions including imprisonment for people found guilty of engaging in same-sex relationships, a ban on all queer advocacy groups, an outlaw of trans health care, and prohibition of same-sex marriages. Ghanaian and transnational human rights organizations have denounced the bill as a violation of human rights, and Archbishop Emeritus Desmond Tutu of South Africa compared the bill to apartheid (Tiernan 2021). As a result of the surge in violence against queer people and people suspected to be LGBTQ+ and sentiments that associate same-sex relationships with deviance, I use pseudonyms for Esther and Sami as well as de-identifiers. Also, out of caution and concern for their safety, Esther and I collaborated on the composite characteristics in these descriptions, as did Tani and Barakesu about how they are represented. I hope these decisions reduce the risk of harm they face. As mentioned earlier, I use pseudonyms for all porters and use locale de-identifiers for Barakesu and Tani.

10. Back then, I was a graduate student who had managed to negotiate through the foreign language exam required for my studies. In my graduate program, students could pass the language requirement through an in-house exam in Spanish, French, or German or by earning a certificate of competency in "a field language." Unfortunately, there were limited opportunities to study African languages in the United States, but Twi was one of the choices available. The politics of African-language learning in the United States means that academic institutions fail to acknowledge, address, or engage how Akan/Twi can function as a hegemonic lingua franca in Accra. Esther's insightful comment about my language skill and translator brought all these tensions into view. At the time, I lacked the resources, institutional support, and capacities to confront and fully address this challenge. This was delicate because, as I mention in earlier chapters, many porters are fluent in two or more languages, spoken primarily outside of the southern regions. Ga and Twi were often tertiary languages for most porters, and they were not spoken with ease. The porters who had started English in school sometimes preferred to speak English. While this preference was rare, English proficiency was seen a status marker and an indicator of schooling.

11. Many conversations take place in multiple languages, including pidgin English, Twi, Konkomba, Lekpokpam, and pidgin Hausa Twi. When a burst of emotion punctuates the dialogue, conversations move between languages, depending on who is in the space. When that happens, I switch on my recorder to record the dialogue and later ask Esther to translate. Given the diversity of languages, it has not been possible to successfully transcribe and translate all idioms and colloquial expressions.

12. A colloquial expression for a place or space that is out of the way or hidden from plain sight and view.

13. There are the change sellers, who charge five pesewas for every one cedi note, but that 5 percent change fee quickly adds up over the course of a day, so most sellers hope their daily sales will suffice in change making.

14. An apt description of the NGO workers who engage in outreach around the markets and typically don brightly colored safety vests bearing the name of their organization as they carry clipboards through the market.

15. This as a reference to a practice where traders in a small town or village will set up stalls on the roadside, hoping that the presence of multiple sellers will attract passing drivers to stop and purchase goods. The downside to this practice was that most of traders were selling the same items, such as palm oil or yams. This meant that, unless the women shared the profits they earned among the group, only one trader out of the six or eight selling would benefit from the sales.

16. Although *body burdens* is a term commonly used by scholars to define the total amount of a substance found in the body, Vanessa Agard-Jones (2015) calls attention to how race, sexuality, and coloniality disproportionally burden and create toxicities in the bodies of Black people in the French Antilles. Agard-Jones's work examines how toxic substances and containments become entangled in social relations. In a similar way, the nook is a site of refuge as well as contamination for the women who sheltered there.

17. In public health and development, the scholarly discourse on sex work and drug use often focuses on harm reduction, risk, and the policy strategies that might best empower head porters (Afriyie, Abass, and Boateng 2016). These important conversations also pathologize or criminalize survival strategies that women and poor people engage in. In this part of the chapter, I am writing toward the possibilities of liberatory practices of harm reduction, defined by Shira Hassan as "a philosophy and set of empowerment-based practices that teach us how to accompany each other as we transform the root causes of harm in our lives" (2022, 43).

18. My use of "Black femme sociality" dances with the dichotomous butch/femme trope of queer identity to embrace how messy ways of being and vague ways of knowing are spaces of emancipatory possibility and feeling.

19. In their "African Studies Keywords: Queer," Kwame Otu and Adriaan van Klinken (2023) outline how *queer* exists in a pentagram of damning tropes and policies of doom on the continent. Cast as an un-African import of the West, queerness is the opposing rationale to facilitate the retrenchment of compulsory heterosexuality.

20. This argument is in conversation with and complementary to Dankwa's (2023) exploration of how the sexual dynamics of women's relationships connect to kinship networks, class identity, and homosocial intimacies.

Chapter 5

1. A wooden sided lorry truck used to transport produce from regional agricultural zones to various commercial markets (Hart 2018).

2. In the United States, *hothead* describes someone who is easily angered or has an explosive temper. In Ghana, *hothead* often refers to someone who is arrogant, brazen, or overconfident.

3. Given the restaurant's location in the state-owned but privately maintained area of Rawlings Square, the private-public aspects of the site are unclear. In the formal section of Makola Market, which accounts for less than half of trade in the area, shops and stalls rely on property managers to negotiate rentals in their spaces. The stalls inside of Makola Market are managed by the state, but stall rentals are managed through intergenerational familial relationships.

4. I have consistently been friendly with the manager or owner of that restaurant, in spite of its numerous name changes and ownership turnovers over the past fifteen years. In its current iteration, the restaurant is owned by Vita, a Ghanaian Lebanese woman whose establishment serves popular Ghanaian dishes, kebabs, and Mediterranean fare. Even though she owns the restaurant and the brand, the owner of the restaurant never owns the actual land on Rawlings Square outright even though, in the last twenty-five years, a restaurant has always occupied the space between two additional eateries.

5. *Aburokyire* means outside of Ghana, foreign, abroad.

6. By the middle of my first year of fieldwork, I had collected a handful of nicknames. Amena's frequently chanted favorite was "Rastabroni," a portmanteau of Rastafarian and *obroni*. The one I liked least was "coconut," which conceptualizes me as (aesthetically and racially) brown on the outside and (ideologically vis-à-vis my geographic origin of the United States) white/foreigner on the inside. In both instances, whiteness is an affective category in hierarchies of difference that has less to do with phenotype but is a signal of passport privilege and access to citizens of the Global North that is expressed in discursive categorizations of race and racialization (Pierre 2012).

7. Sometimes called a "gub'ment" or "gov'a'ment" name, the term *government name* describes or refers to a person's name on legal documents, such as a birth certificate and social security card, as opposed to the name the person might be more commonly associated with.

8. Restaurants, like trade space at Makola, are part of a network of subleases operated and maintained by the AMA, which regulates the area as part of its jurisdiction over the city. The corner was an ethnographic sweet spot; it held a vantage view of the sidewalk sales areas outside the park walls, and I could easily observe the trucks and buses parked on the square and see the hurried shuttling of pedestrians moving through Makola.

9. Enclosed stores with sliding-glass windows and air-conditioning are seen as more high end and expensive. Fusena's recommendation is an analysis of the way English is viewed as a mark of high cultural and social capital.

10. When the women refer to the Sakina and her friends as "Five Milly," it is a synonym for ¢500. In 2007, the Bank of Ghana instituted a redenomination of the cedis where four zeroes were deleted from the currency. From July to December 2007, the Bank of Ghana carried out the redenomination, exchanging the old ¢10,000 for the current GH¢1. During this period, both the old and new currencies were in circulation until January 1, 2008. In common parlance, especially outside of the capital, people will colloquially use the term *one million* to describe GH¢100.

11. I have steered away from ethnicity as a conceptual framework to resist reanimating intellectual shortcuts to "ethnic conflict," which I argue is a Trojan horse trotted out in academic discourse on Africa as the primordial source of conflict rather than as an output of coloniality.

REFERENCES

Acheampong, Kwame. 2017. "2017 Budget: Gov't Abolishes 'Kayayei Tax.'" *StarrFM*, March 2, 2017. https://starrfm.com.gh/2017/03/2017-budget-govt-abolishes-kayayei-tax.

Adamu, Zaina. 2020. "How Ghana's Black Lives Matter Solidarity Protest Ended with Clashes with the Police." *CNN*, June 15, 2020. https://www.cnn.com/2020/06/15/africa/ghana-protests-black-lives-matter/index.html.

ADM (Accra Daily Mail). 2005. "10,000 'Kayayei' in Accra." *GhanaWeb*, Regional News, April 4, 2005. http://www.ghanaweb.com/GhanaHomePage/NewsArchive/artikel.php?ID=78611.

Adom, Komla. 2016. "What's in a Legacy? Rawlings Chain, Kufuor Gallon, Mahama Camboo, Akufo-Addo...?" *Modern Ghana*, December 29, 2016. https://www.modernghana.com/news/745835/whats-in-a-legacy-rawlings-chain-kufuor-gallon-mahama-ca.html.

Afful, Joseph Benjamin Archibald. 2006. "Address Terms Among University Students in Ghana: A Case Study." *Languages and Intercultural Communication* 1 (1): 76–91.

Afriyie, Kwadwo, Kabila Abass, and Micheal Boateng. 2016. "A Journey to the South: Socio-economic Implications for Young Female Head Porters in the Central Business District of Kumasi, Ghana." *International Journal of Migration and Residential Mobility* 1 (2): 176–94.

Agard-Jones, Vanessa. 2015. "Case: Chlordécone." Presented at "The Manufacturing of Rights," Beirut, May 14–16, 2015. YouTube video, 14:49. https://www.youtube.com/watch?v=yvqVkR4Iuqs.

Agarwal, Seema, Memunatu Attah, Nana Apt, Margaret Grieco, E. A. Kwakye, and Jeff Turner. 1997. "Bearing the Weight: The Kayayoo, Ghana's Working Girl Child." *International Social Work* 40 (3): 245–63.

Agbola, Ruby Melody. 2013. "Does Total Quality Management Affect the Performance of Small and Medium Enterprises? A Case of Manufacturing SMEs in Ghana." *World Applied Sciences Journal* 28. https://doi.org/10.5829/idosi.wasj.2013.28.efmo.27001.

Ahmed, Sara. 2004. "Collective Feelings; or, The Impressions Left by Others." *Theory, Culture & Society* 21 (2): 25–42.

———. 2006. *Queer Phenomenology: Orientations, Objects, Others.* Durham, NC: Duke University Press.

———. 2010. *The Cultural Politics of Emotions.* London: Routledge.

Aidoo, Ama Ata. 1977. *Our Sister Killjoy; or, Reflections from a Black-Eyed Squint.* New York: NOK Publishers International.

Akurang-Parry, Kwabena Opare. 2000. "Colonial Forced Labor Policies for Road-Building in Southern Ghana and International Anti-Forced Labor Pressures, 1900–1940." *African Economic History* 28:1–25.

Akyeampong, Emmanuel, and Hippolyte Fofack. 2014. "The Contribution of African Women to Economic Growth and Development in the Pre-colonial and Colonial Period: Historical

Perspectives and Policy Implications." *Economic History of Developing Regions* 29 (1): 42–73.

Alleyne, Osei. 2017. "Dancehall Diaspora: Roots, Routes & Reggae Music in Ghana." PhD diss., University of Pennsylvania.

Allman, Jean. 1996. "Rounding Up Spinsters: Gender Chaos and Unmarried Women in Colonial Asante." *Journal of African History* 37 (2): 195–214.

———. 2019 "#HerskovitsMustFall? A Meditation on Whiteness, African Studies, and the Unfinished Business of 1968." *African Studies Review* 62 (3): 6–39.

Amadiume, Ifi. 1987. *Male Daughters, Female Husbands: Gender and Sex in an African Society.* London: Zed Books.

Andersson, Helene. 2016. "Colonial Urban Legacies: An Analysis of Socio-spatial Structures in Accra, Ghana." Bachelor's thesis, Uppsala University.

Anquandah, James Kwesi. 2018. "An Interview with James Kwesi Anquandah." By Rachel Ama Asaa Engmann. *African Archaeological Review* 35:379–91.

Anquandah, James, Benjamin Kankpeyeng, and Wazi Apoh, eds. 2014. *Current Perspectives on Archaeology in Ghana.* Legon-Accra, Ghana: University of Ghana / Sub-Saharan Publishers.

Ansah, Gladys Nyarko, Jemima Asabea Anderson, Suleman Alhassan Anamzoya, and Fidelia Ohemeng. 2017. "'Bra, Sɛn, Yɛnkɔ . . . That Is All I Know in Akan': How Female Migrants from Rural North Survive with Minimal Bilingualism in Urban Markets in Ghana." *Ghana Journal of Linguistics* 6 (1): 49–74.

Ansah, Stephen. 2021. "Kaaka's Murder: Gunshots as Angry Youth Clash with Police." *Riddims Ghana,* June 29, 2021. Accessed July 1, 2021. https://riddimsghana.com/news/kaakas-murder-gunshots-as-angry-youth-clash-with-police/.

Anumo, Felogene, and Awuor Onyango. 2020. "Embodying Protest: Feminist Organizing in Kenya." In *Gender, Protests and Political Change in Africa,* edited by Awino Okech, 201–24. London: Palgrave Macmillan.

Apawu, Emefa. 2021. "We Need Modernised Market Structures and Systems for 'Kayayei'— Otiko Djaba." *JoyOnline,* December 25, 2021. https://www.myjoyonline.com/we-need-modernised-market-structures-and-systems-for-kayayei-otiko-djaba/.

Apoh, Wazi, James Anquandah, and Seyram Amenyo-Xa. 2019. "Shit, Blood, Artifacts, and Tears: Interrogating Visitor Perception and Archaeological Residues at Ghana's Cape Castle Slave Dungeon." *Journal of African Diaspora Archaeology and Heritage* 7 (2): 105–30. https://doi.org/10.1080/21619441.2018.1578480.

Aremu, Johnson Olaosebikan, and Adeyinka Theresa Ajayi. 2014. "Expulsion of Nigerian Immigrant Community from Ghana in 1969: Causes and Impact." *Developing Country Studies* 4 (10): 176–86.

Arjona, Jamie M. 2017. "Homesick Blues: Excavating Crooked Intimacies in Late Nineteenth- and Early Twentieth-Century Jook Joints." *Historical Archaeology* 51:43–59.

Arthur, Isaac. 2018. "Exploring the Development Prospects of Accra Airport City." *Area Development and Policy* 1–16, https://doi.org/10.1080/23792949.2018.1428112.

Asante Market Women. 1982. Directed by Claudia Milne, with anthropologist Charlotte Boaiety. *Disappearing World,* season 1, episode 25. Aired March 16, 1982, on Granada Television, UK.

Asare, Kwaku. 2019. "Ghana's Year of Return: Citizenship Without Political Rights." Ghana Center for Democratic Development (blog), July 1, 2019. https://cddgh.org/ghanas-year-of-return-citizenship-without-political-rights.

Asiedu, Kwasi Gyamfi. 2020. "After George Floyd, Ghana's Simple Message to African Americans: 'Come Home.'" *Quartz Africa,* June 20, 2020. https://qz.com/africa/1871352/george-floyd-ghana-message-to-african-americans-come-home.

Asiedu, Alex, and Samuel Agyei-Mensah. 2008. "Traders on the Run: Activities of Street Vendors in the Accra Metropolitan Area, Ghana." *Norsk Geografisk Tidsskrift—Norweigan Journal of Geography* 62 (3): 191–202.

Asomaning, Vida, Fred Amposah, Memunatu Attah, Nana Apt, and Margaret Grieco. 1996. "Bearing the Weight: The Centrality of Head Loading in a Petty Trading Structure." In *At Christmas and on Rainy Days: Transport, Travel and the Female Traders of Accra*, edited by Margaret Grieco, Nana Apt, and Jeff Turner, 59–81. Aldershot, UK: Avebury Press.

Asuro, Salifu A. 2015. "The Morphology of Contemporary Ghanaian Pidgin English." *African Journal of Applied Research* 1 (1): 345–62.

Attah, Ayesha Harruna. 2019. *The Hundred Wells of Salaga*. New York: Other Press.

Awachie, Ifeanyi. 2020. "Archiving the African Feminist Festival Through Oral Communication and Social Media." *Feminist Review* 125 (1): 88–93.

Awal, Mohammed. 2019. "After 'Year of Return' This Is How Ghana Plans to Attract More Investors." *Face2Face Africa*, December 31, 2019. https://face2faceafrica.com/article/after-year-of -return-this-is-how-ghana-plans-to-attract-more-investors.

Awedoba, A. K. 2006. *The Peoples of Northern Ghana*. Accra, Ghana: National Commission on Culture.

Awedoba, Albert Kanlisi, and Stephen Owoahene-Acheampong. 2017. "What Is in a Nickname: Ghanaian Nickname Cultures." *OGIRISI: A New Journal of African Studies* 13. https://doi .org/10.4314/og.v13i1.8.

Bailey, Moya. 2021. *Misogynoir Transformed: Black Women's Digital Resistance*. New York: New York University Press.

Bakhtin, Mikail. 1984. *Problems of Dostoevsky's Poetics*. Edited and translated by Caryl Emerson. Minneapolis: University of Minnesota Press.

Battle-Baptiste, Whitney. 2010. "Global Conversations." *Museum International* 62 (1–2): 26–30.

Bayor, Justin. 2007. "Ghana: No Vocational School in the North to Train Girls Migrating to the South." *Public Agenda*, December 10, 2007. https://allafrica.com/stories/200712101407.html.

Beliso-De Jesús, Aisha M., and Jemima Pierre. 2019. "Anthropology of White Supremacy." *American Anthropologist* 122 (1): 65–75.

Benke, Falk. 2016. "Driving Change: The Story of Miss Taxi—One of Ghana's First Female Taxi Drivers." *Medium*, Ghanaian Entrepreneurs no. 4, April 11, 2016. https://medium.com /beam-blog/driving-change-the-story-ofmiss-taxi-one-of-ghana-s-first-female-taxi -drivers-42e98deeff81.

Bennett, Jane, and Charmaine Pereira, eds. 2013. *Jacketed Women: Qualitative Research Methods on Sexualities and Gender in Africa*. Claremont, South Africa: University of Cape Town Press.

Bentsi-Enchill, Nii K. 1979. "Losing Illusions at Makola Market." *West Africa*, September 3, 1979, 1589–92.

Beoku-Betts, Josephine. 2005. "Western Perceptions of African Women in the 19th and Early 20th Centuries." In *Readings in Gender in Africa*, edited by Andrea Cornwall, 20–25. Oxford: James Currey.

Berlant, Lauren. 2011. *Cruel Optimism*. Durham, NC: Duke University Press.

Berry, Maya J., Claudia Chávez Argüelles, Shanya Cordis, Sarah Ihmoud, and Elizabeth Velásquez Estrada. 2017. "Toward a Fugitive Anthropology: Gender, Race, and Violence in the Field." *Cultural Anthropology* 32 (4): 537–65. https://doi.org/10.14506/ca32.4.05.

Biney, Ama. 2014. "The Historical Discourse on African Humanism." In *Ubuntu: Curating the Archive*, edited by Leonhard Praeg and Siphokazi Magadla, 27–53. Scottsville, South Africa: University of KwaZulu-Natal Press.

Blay, Yaba Amgborale. 2008. "All the 'Africans' Are Men, All the 'Sistas' Are 'American,' but Some of Us Resist: Realizing African Feminism(s) as an Africological Research Methodology." *Journal of Pan African Studies* 2 (2): 58–73.

Bloom, Peter J., Stephan F. Miescher, and Takyiwaa Manuh, eds. 2014. *Modernization as Spectacle in Africa*. Bloomington: Indiana University Press.

Boakye-Boaten, Agya. 2008. "Street Children: Experiences from the Streets of Accra." *Research Journal of International Studies* 8:76–84.

Bolles, Lynn. 2020. "Reciprocal Arrangements: The Life Story of 'Rosalind'—Woman Worker, Mother, and Jamaican." *Feminist Anthropology* 1 (2): 260–71.

Boswell, Rosabelle. 2017. "Sensuous Stories in the Indian Ocean Islands." *Senses and Society* 12 (2): 193–208.

Bowan, Lorraine. 2013. "Polygamy and Patriarchy: An Intimate Look at Marriage in Ghana Through a Human Rights Lens." *Contemporary Journal of African Studies* 1 (2). https://hdl .handle.net/10520/EJC147094.

Bowles, Laurian R. 2016. "Dress Politics and Framing Self in Ghana: The Studio Photographs of Felicia Abban." *African Arts* 49 (4): 48–57.

———. 2021. "Black Feminist Ethnography and the Racial Politics of Porter Labor in Ghana." *Feminist Anthropology* 2 (1): 65–77.

brown, adrienne maree. 2019. *Pleasure Activism: The Politics of Feeling Good*. Chico, CA: AK Press.

Brown, DeNeen L. 2021. "'Uncomfortable Truth': The New Push for a Slavery Reparations Commission in Congress." *Washington Post*, February 10, 2021. https://www.washingtonpost.com /history/2021/02/10/reparations-slavery-congress-hearing-commission.

Browne, Simone. 2015. *Dark Matters: On the Surveillance of Blackness*. Durham, NC: Duke University Press.

Brukum, N. J. K. 2003. "The Voices of the Elite in Northern Ghana, 1918–1938." *Transactions of the Historical Society of Ghana*, n.s., no. 7, 271–81.

Bulmuo, Bruce Misbahu. 2014. "Abolish Tax on Kayayei." *GhanaWeb*, Regional News, July 18, 2014. https://www.ghanaweb.com/GhanaHomePage/NewsArchive/Abolish-tax-on-kayayei-317452.

Bunster B., Ximena. 1977. "Talking Pictures: Field Method and Visual Mode." *Signs: Journal of Women in Culture and Society* 3 (1): 278–93. https://doi.org/10.1086/493459.

Caldwell, Kia Lilly. 2003. "'Look at Her Hair': The Body Politics of Black Womanhood in Brazil." *Transforming Anthropology* 11 (2): 18–29.

Cammaert, Jessica. 2016. *Undesirable Practices: Women, Children, and the Politics of the Body in Northern Ghana, 1930–1972*. Lincoln: University of Nebraska Press.

Campt, Tina M. 2017. *Listening to Images*. Durham, NC: Duke University Press.

———. 2019. "Black Visuality and the Practice of Refusal." *Women and Performance: A Journal of Feminist Theory* 29 (1): 79–87.

Cerwonka, Allaine, and Liisa H. Malkki. 2008. *Improvising Theory: Process and Temporality in Ethnographic Fieldwork*. Chicago: University of Chicago Press.

Chamlee-Wright, Emily. 2002. *The Cultural Foundations of Economic Development: Urban Female Entrepreneurship in Ghana*. London: Routledge.

Christian, Barbara. 1988. "The Race for Theory." *Feminist Studies* 14 (1): 67–79.

Citi Newsroom. 2021. "Demolition of 3-Storey Building Gutted by Fire at Makola Market Begins." August 23, 2021. https://citinewsroom.com/2021/08/demolition-of-3-storey-building -gutted-by-fire-at-makola-market-begins/.

Clark, Gracia. 1994. *Onions Are My Husband: Survival and Accumulation by West African Market Women*. Chicago: University of Chicago Press.

Collins, Patricia Hill. 2004. *Black Sexual Politics: African Americans, Gender and the New Racism*. Boston: Taylor and Francis.

Cox, Aimee Meredith. 2015. *Shapeshifters: Black Girls and the Choreography of Citizenship*. Durham, NC: Duke University Press.

Dako, Kari. 2002. "Pidgin as a Gender Specific Language in Ghana." *Ghanaian Journal of English Studies* 1 (1): 72–82.

Dangarembga, Tsitsi. 1988. *Nervous Conditions*. London: Women's Press.

Dankwa, Serena Owusua. 2021. *Knowing Women: Same-Sex Intimacy, Gender, and Identity in Postcolonial Ghana*. Cambridge: Cambridge University Press.

Darkwah, Akosua K. 2007. "Making Hay While the Sun Shines: Ghanaian Female Traders and Their Insertion in the Global Economy." In *The Gender of Globalization: Women Navigating Cultural and Economic Marginalities*, edited by Nandini Gunewardena and Ann Kingsolver, 61–83. Oxford: James Currey.

Darkwah, Akosua K., and Akosua Adomako Ampofo. 2008. "Race, Gender and Global Love: Non-Ghanaian Wives, Insiders or Outsiders in Ghana?" *International Journal of Sociology of the Family* 34 (2): 187–208. http://www.jstor.org/stable/23070751.

Davis, Dána-Ain. 2024. "Traumatic Repercussions: Black Women and Obstetric Racism," Public Lecture, UC Berkeley. March 7.

Davis, Dána-Ain, and Christa Craven. 2016. *Feminist Ethnography: Thinking Through Methodologies, Challenges, and Possibilities*. Lanham, MD: Rowman and Littlefield.

Decker, Alicia C., and Gabeda Baderoon. 2018. "African Feminisms: Cartographies for the Twenty-First Century." *Meridians* 17 (2): 219–31.

de Laat, Sonya, and Valérie Gorin. 2016. "Iconographies of Humanitarian Aid in Africa." In *Learning from the Past to Shape the Future: Lessons from the History of Humanitarian Action in Africa*, edited by Christina Bennett, Matthew Foley, and Hanna B. Krebs, 15–30. HPG Working Paper. London: Humanitarian Policy Group, Overseas Development Institute. https://cdn.odi.org/media/documents/11148.pdf#page=19.

Der, Benedict G. 1998. *The Slave Trade in Northern Ghana*. Accra, Ghana: Woeli Publishing Services.

Diwakar, Dheeraj. 2021. "Promotion of Proper Human Sexual Rights and Ghanaian Family Values Bill Makes LGBTQ+ Community Illegal." *Jurist: Legal News and Commentary*, August 23, 2021. https://www.jurist.org/commentary/2021/08/dheeraj-diwakar-human-sexual-rights-bill-ghana-lgbtq-illegal.

Ebron, Paulla A. 2007. *Performing Africa*. Princeton, NJ: Princeton University Press.

Eke, Peter P. 1990. "Social Anthropology and Two Contrasting Uses of Tribalism in Africa." *Comparative Studies in Society and History* 32 (4): 660–700.

Engelke, Matthew. 2010. "Past Pentecostalism: Notes on Rupture, Realignment, and Everyday Life of Pentecostal and African Independent Churches." *Africa* 80 (2): 177–99.

Enwezor, Okwui. 2010. "Modernity and Postcolonial Ambivalence." *South Atlantic Quarterly* 109 (3): 595–620.

Essel, Isaac. 2009. "Kayayei on Strike; Protest Against Mass Eviction." *ModernGhana*, September 9, 2009. https://www.modernghana.com/news/237286/1/kayayei-on-strike-protest-against-mass-eviction.html.

Evans-Pritchard, E.E. 1940. *The Nuer: A Description of the Modes of Livelihood and Political Institutions of a Nilotic People*. Oxford: Clarendon Press.

FAO (Food and Agriculture Organization of the United Nations). n.d. "FAO in Ghana: Ghana at a Glance." Accessed June 15, 2021. http://www.fao.org/ghana/fao-in-ghana/ghana-at-a-glance/en.

Fiereck, Kirk, Neville Hoad, and Danai S. Muposta. 2020. "A Queering-to-Come." *GLQ: A Journal of Lesbian and Gay Studies* 26 (3): 363–76.

Finch, Aisha K. 2022. "Introduction: Black Feminism and the Practice of Care." *Palimpsest: A Journal on Women, Gender and the Black International* 11 (1): 1–41.

Fraker, Anne, and Barbara Harrell-Bond. 1979. "Feminine Influence." *West Africa*, November 26, 1979, 2182–87.

Fortes, M and E.E. Evans-Pritchard, eds. 1940. *African Political Systems*. London: Oxford University Press.

Germansky, Julie Faye. 2017. "Why You Should Visit Ghana, the Gem of West Africa." *Intrepid*, May 21, 2017. https://www.intrepidtravel.com/adventures/ghana-travel-guide.

Getz, Trevor. 2004. *Slavery and Reform in West Africa: Towards Emancipation in Nineteenth-Century Senegal and the Gold Coast*. Athens: Ohio University Press.

Ghanaian Times. 2023. "DuBois Centre To Be Redeveloped Into Museum Complex." August 29. https://www.myjoyonline.com/du-bois-centre-to-be-redeveloped-into-museum-complex/

GhanaWeb TV. 2021. "GNFS Gives Reasons for Delay in Fighting Makola Fire." July 5, 2021. YouTube video, 3:54. https://www.youtube.com/watch?v=TAI96aW6XIU.

Gilliam, Angela. 1998. "The Brazilian *Mulata*: Images in the Global Economy." *Race & Class* 40 (1): 57–69.

Gilroy, Paul. 1993. *The Black Atlantic: Modernity and Double Consciousness*. Cambridge, MA: Harvard University Press.

GNA (Ghana News Agency). 2009. "10,800 'Kayayeis' Get Free Health Care." September 18, 2009. https://www.modernghana.com/news/239578/1/10800-kayayeis-get-free-health-care.html.

———. 2020. "Ministry of Tourism to Preserve Legacy of W. E. B. Du Bois." October 20, 2020. https://www.ghanaweb.com/GhanaHomePage/entertainment/Ministry-of-Tourism-to-preserve-legacy-of-W-E-B-Du-Bois-1086412.

Goody, Jack. 1995. *The Expansive Moment: Anthropology in Britain and Africa, 1918–1970*. Cambridge: Cambridge University Press.

Graphic Online. 2023. "Accra: Kayayeis Benefit from Reflo Company Sanitary Pads Donation." October 24, 2023. https://www.graphic.com.gh/news/general-news/accra-kayayeis-benefit-from-reflo-company-sanitary-pads-donation.html.

Greene, Sandra. 2011. *West African Narratives of Slavery: Texts from Late Nineteenth- and Early Twentieth-Century Ghana*. Bloomington: Indiana University Press.

Grieco, Margaret, Nana Apt, and Jeff Turner, eds. 1996. *At Christmas and on Rainy Days: Transport, Travel and the Female Traders of Accra*. Aldershot, UK: Avebury Press.

Grier, Beverly. 1992. "Pawns, Porters, and Petty Traders: Women in the Transition to Cash Crop Agriculture in Colonial Ghana." *Signs: Journal of Women in Culture and Society* 17 (2): 304–28.

Gumbonzvanda, Nyaradzayi, Farirai Gumbonzvanda, and RochelleAnn Burgess. 2021. "Decolonising the 'Safe Space' as an African Innovation: The Nhanga as Quiet Activism to Improve Women's Health and Wellbeing." *Critical Public Health* 31 (2): 169–81.

Gwaltney, John Langston. 1980. *Drylongso: A Self-Portrait of Black America*. New York: Random House.

Hagan, Ampson. 2019. "On Not Looking Like an Expert: Being Black and Doing Research in Africa, White People's Historical and Theoretical Turf." *Footnotes: Multimodal. Anticolonial. Iconoclastic* (blog), April 29, https://footnotesblogcom.wordpress.com/2019/04/29/guest-post-on-not-looking-like-an-expert-being-black-and-doing-research-in-africa-white-peoples-historical-and-theoretical-turf/.

Hammond, Evelynn M. 1997. "Toward a Genealogy of Black Female Sexuality: The Problematic of Silence." In *Feminist Genealogies, Colonial Legacies, and Democratic Futures*, edited by M. Jacqui Alexander and Chandra Talpade Mohanty, 170–82. New York: Routledge.

Hanrahan, Kelsey B. 2015. "'Mɔn' (to Marry/to Cook): Negotiating Becoming a Wife and Woman in the Kitchens of a Northern Ghanaian Konkomba Community." *Gender, Place & Culture* 22 (9): 1323–39.

Harper, Douglas. 1987. "The Visual Ethnographic Narrative." *Visual Anthropology* 1 (1): 1–19.

Harrison, Faye V. 2007. "Feminist Methodology as a Tool for Ethnographic Inquiry on Globalization." In *The Gender of Globalization: Women Navigating Cultural and Economic Mar-*

ginalities, edited by Nandini Gunewardena and Ann Kingsolver, 23–31. Santa Fe, NM: School for Advanced Research Press.

———. 2016. "Decolonizing Anthropology: A Conversation with Faye V. Harrison, Part I." *Savage Minds*, May 2, 2016. https://savageminds.org/2016/05/02/decolonizing-anthropology-a-conversation-with-faye-v-harrison-part-i.

Hart, Jennifer. 2016. *Ghana on the Go: African Mobility in the Age of Motor Transportation.* Bloomington: Indiana University Press.

———. 2018. "African Automobility: Mammy Trucks in Twentieth-Century Ghana." *T2M: Transport, Traffic and Mobility.* November 12. https://t2m.org/african-automobility-mammy-trucks-in-twentieth-century-ghana/

———. 2024. *Making an African City: Technopolitics and the Infrastructure of Everyday Life in Colonial Accra.* Bloomington: Indiana University Press.

Hartman, Saidiya. 2008. *Lose Your Mother: A Journey Along the Atlantic Slave Route.* New York: Macmillan.

Harvey, Andrew S., and Maria Elena Taylor. 2000. "Time Use." In *Designing Household Survey Questionnaires for Developing Countries: Lessons from 15 Years of the Living Standards Measurement Study*, vol. 2, edited by Margaret Grosh and Paul Glewwe, 249–73. Washington, DC: World Bank.

Hassan, Shira. 2022. *Saving Our Own Lives: A Liberatory Practice of Harm Reduction.* Chicago: Haymarket Books.

Holsey, Bayo. 2008. *Routes of Remembrance: Refashioning the Slave Trade in Ghana.* Chicago: University of Chicago Press.

———. 2013. "Black Atlantic Visions: History, Race, and Transnationalism in Ghana." *Cultural Anthropology* 28 (3): 504–18.

Honwana, Alcinda M. 2012. *The Time of Youth: Work, Social Change, and Politics in Africa.* Hartford, CT: Kumerian Press.

hooks, bell. 1989. "From *Black Is a Woman's Color.*" *Callaloo* 39 (Spring): 382–88.

———. 1991. "Black Women Intellectuals." In *Breaking Bread: Insurgent Black Intellectual Life*, by bell hooks and Cornel West, 147–64. Boston: South End Press.

———. 2014. "Are You Still a Slave? Liberating the Black Female Body." Eugene Lang College, New School, New York, May 6, 2014. YouTube video, 1:55:32. https://www.youtube.com/watch?v=rJk0hNROvzs.

House-Midamba, Bessie, and Felix K. Ekechi, eds. 1995. *African Market Women and Economic Power: The Role of Women in African Economic Development.* Westport, CT: Greenwood Press.

Huck, Nichole. 2007. "Ending Kayayoo in the North." Blog post. Radion Station Justice FM. November 18. https://www.travelblog.org/africa/ghana/northern/tamale/blog-220717.

Hurston, Zora Neale. 1937. *Their Eyes Were Watching God.* Philadelphia: J. B. Lippincott.

Imam, Haruna Abdalla, and Hardy Tamimu. 2015. "'Life Beyond the Walls of My Hometown': Social Safety Networks as a Coping Strategy for Northern Migrants in Accra." *Asian Journal of Social Sciences and Management Studies* 2 (1): 25–43.

Jackson, Zakiyyah. 2020. *Becoming Human: Matter and Meaning in an Antiblack World.* New York: New York University Press.

Jili, Bulelani. 2022. "The Specter of Hobbes and Other White Men in African Anthropology." *Fieldsights*, April 14, 2022, Member Voices section. https://culanth.org/fieldsights/the-specter-of-hobbes-and-other-white-men-in-african-anthropology.

Johnson, Jessica Marie. 2020. *Wicked Flesh: Black Women, Intimacy and Freedom in the Atlantic World.* Philadelphia: University of Pennsylvania Press.

Johnson, Marion.1986. "The Slaves of Salaga." *Journal of African History* 27 (2): 341–62.

Joy News. 2021. "Social Media Users Peeved About Fire Service Delay to Douse Fire at Makola Market." July 5, 2021. https://www.myjoyonline.com/social-media-users-peeved-about-fire-service-delay-to-douse-fire-at-makola-market.

Kagumire, Rosebell. 2020. "Black Lives Matter Resonates with Africans Pushing for Decolonization." *Global Reporting Centre* (website), editorial, June 29, 2020. https://globalreportingcentre.org/ideas/black-lives-matter-resonates-with-africans.

Kambala, Iddrisu Mohammed. 2022. "Northern Ghana Is Underdeveloped Because of Underinvestment During Colonial Rule, Not Geography." *The Conversation*, September 27, 2022. https://theconversation.com/northern-ghana-is-underdeveloped-because-of-underinvestment-during-colonial-rule-not-geography-190795?s=09.

Kankpeyeng, Benjamin. 2009. "The Slave Trade in Northern Ghana: Landmarks, Legacies and Connections." *Slavery & Abolition* 30 (2): 209–21. https://doi.org/10.1080/01440390902818930.

Keeling, Kara. 2007. *The Witch's Flight: The Cinematic, the Black Femme, and the Image of Common Sense.* Durham, NC: Duke University Press.

Kobo, Ousman. 2010. "'We Are Citizens Too': The Politics of Citizenship in Independent Ghana." *Journal of Modern African Studies* 48 (1): 67–94.

Kuba, Richard, and Carola Lentz. 2020. "The Dagara and Their Neighbors (Burkina Faso and Ghana)." *EJAB: Electronic Journal of Africana Bibliography* 7. https://doi.org/10.52214/ejab.v7i.6981.

Kudoto, Donatella. 2021. "Girl Guides to Train 100 Kayayei." *Graphic Online*, November 18, 2021. https://www.graphic.com.gh/news/general-news/girl-guides-to-train-100-kayayei.

Lentz, Carola. 2006. *Ethnicity and the Making of History in Northern Ghana.* Edinburgh: Edinburgh University Press.

Lewis, Desiree. 2011. "Representing African Sexualities." In *African Sexualities: A Reader,* edited by Sylvia Tamale, 198–216. Cape Town: Pambakuza Press.

Little, Peter. 2021. *Burning Matters: Life, Labor and E-Waste Pyropolitics in Ghana.* Oxford University Press.

Lorde, Audre. 1984. "Uses of the Erotic: The Erotic as Power." In *Sister Outsider: Essays and Speeches,* 53–59. Freedom, CA: Crossing Press.

Macharia, Keguro. 2019. *Frottage: Frictions of Intimacy Across the Black Diaspora.* New York: New York University Press.

Mafeje, Archie. 1998. "Anthropology and Independent Africans: Suicide or End of an Era?" *African Sociological Review* 2 (1): 1–43.

Mama, Amina. 2001. "Challenging Subjects: Gender and Power in African Contexts." Plenary Address, Nordic Africa Institute Conference "Beyond Identity: Rethinking Power in Africa," Upsala, October 4–7, 2001. *African Sociological Review* 5 (2): 63–73.

Mampane, Tumi. 2022. "This Field I Call Home: Black Feminist (Auto)Ethnography in Alexandra Township, South Africa." *African Identities* 22 (3): 570–83. https://doi.org/10.1080/14725843.2022.2082378.

Manful, Kuukuwa O. 2022. "Research with African Adolescents: Critical Epistemologies and Methodological Considerations." *African Affairs* 121 (484): 467–85.

Manoukian, Madeline. (1951) 2017. *Tribes of the Northern Territories of the Gold Coast.* London: International African Institute. Reprint, London: Routledge.

Matebeni, Zethu. 2013. "Intimacy, Queerness, Race." *Cultural Studies* 27 (3): 414–17.

McClaurin, Irma, ed. 2001. *Black Feminist Anthropology: Theory, Politics, Praxis, and Poetics.* New Brunswick, NJ: Rutgers University Press.

McDonald, Briana. 2019. "A Review of *The Hundred Wells of Salaga* by Ayesha Harruna Attah." *Literary Review.* Accessed January 4, 2021. https://www.theliteraryreview.org/book-review/a-review-of-the-hundred-wells-of-salaga-by-ayesha-harruna-attah.

McFadden, Patricia. 2003. "Sexual Pleasure as Feminist Choice." *Feminist Africa*, no. 2, 50–60.

———. 2018. "Contemporarity: Sufficiency in a Radical African Feminist Life." *Meridians: Feminisms, Race, Transnationalism* 17 (2): 415–31.

McKinley, Catherine E. 2021. *The African Lookbook: A Visual History of 100 Years of African Women*. New York: Bloomsbury.

McKittrick, Katherine. 2006. *Demonic Grounds: Black Women and the Cartographies of Struggle*. Minneapolis: University of Minnesota Press.

Mead, Margaret. 2009. "Visual Anthropology in a Discipline of Words." In *Principles of Visual Anthropology*, 3rd ed., edited by Paul Hockings, 1–10. Berlin: De Gruyter Mouton. https://doi.org/10.1515/9783110221138.1.

Merleau-Ponty, Maurice. 2011. *Phenomenology of Perception*. Translated by Donald A. Landes. London: Routledge.

Meyer, Birgit. 1998. "'Make a Complete Break with the Past': Memory and Post-Colonial Modernity in Ghanaian Pentecostalist Discourse." *Journal of Religions in Africa* 28 (3): 316–49.

———. 2008. "Mami Water as a Christian Demon: The Eroticism of Forbidden Pleasures in Southern Ghana." In *Sacred Waters: Arts for Mami Wata and Other Divinities in Africa and the Diaspora*, edited by Henry John Drewal, 383–98. Bloomington: Indiana University Press.

Miescher, Stephan F., Peter J. Bloom, and Takyiwaa Manuh. 2014. "Introduction." In *Modernization as Spectacle in Africa*, edited by Peter J. Bloom, Stephan F. Miescher, and Takyiwaa Manuh, 1–16. Bloomington: Indiana University Press.

Mohammed, Wunpini Fatimata. 2020. "What COVID-19 Reveals About Educational Inequality in Ghana." *Al Jazeera*, April 7, 2020. https://www.aljazeera.com/features/2020/4/7/what-covid-19-reveals-about-educational-inequality-in-ghana.

Morgan, Joan. 2015. "Why We Get Off: Moving Towards a Black Feminist Politics of Pleasure." *Black Scholar* 45 (4): 36–46.

Morrison, Amani. 2018. "Black Hair Haptics: Touch and Transgressing the Black Female Body." *Meridians: Feminisms, Race, Transnationalism* 17 (1): 82–96.

Moultrie, Monique. 2018. "Putting a Ring on It: Black Women, Black Churches, and Coerced Monogamy." *Black Theology* 16 (3): 231–47. https://doi.org/10.1080/14769948.2018.1492304.

Mulla, Sameena. 2011. "Facing Victims: Forensics, Visual Technologies, and Sexual Assault Examination." *Medical Anthropology* 30 (3): 271–94.

Mullings, Leith. 2008. "Race and Globalization: Racialization from Below." In *Transnational Blackness: Navigating the Global Color Line*, edited by Manning Marable and Vanessa Agard-Jones, 1–19. New York: Palgrave Macmillan.

Muposta, Danai. 2010. "If I Could Write This in Fire: African Feminist Ethics for Research in Africa." In "Agenda Africa: (Re)imagining African Studies," special issue, *Postamble* 6 (1): 1–18.

Murdock, George Peter. 1959. *Africa: Its Peoples and Their Culture History*. New York: McGraw-Hill.

Musangi, Neo Sinoxolo. 2018. "Homing with My Mother / How Women in My Family Married Women." *Meridians: Feminisms, Race, Transnationalism* 17 (2): 401–14.

Narfra, Yao Eli Sebastian. 2024. "The Dynamics of Head Porters (Kayayei) In Accra and (Paa Oo Paa) In Kumasi: A Generational Challenge." *The Ghana Report*. August 21. https://www.theghanareport.com/the-dynamics-of-head-porters-kayayei-in-accra-and-paa-oo-paa-in-kumasi-a-generational-challenge/

Nhemachena, Artwell, and Tapiwa Victor Warikandwa, eds. 2019. *From African Peer Review Mechanisms to African Queer Review Mechanisms? Robert Gabriel Mugabe, Empire and the Decolonisation of African Orifices*. Bamenda, Cameroon: Langaa RPCIG.

Nyabor, Jonas. 2019. "Anas Exposes AMA Taskforce Who Seize Goods, Extort Money from Makola Market Traders." *Citi Newsroom*, December 2, 2019. https://citinewsroom.com/2019/12/anas-exposes-ama-taskforce-who-seize-goods-extort-money-from-makola-market-traders.

Nyanzi, Stella. 2013. "Dismantling Reified African Culture Through Localised Homosexualities in Uganda." *Culture, Health & Sexuality* 15 (8): 952–67.

———. 2020. "Personal Narrative: Bloody Precarious Activism in Uganda." In *The Palgrave Handbook of Critical Menstruation Studies*, edited by Chris Bobel et al., 551–59. Singapore: Palgrave Macmillan. https://doi.org/10.1007/978-981-15-0614-7_42.

Obeng-Odoom, Franklin. 2010. "'Abnormal' Urbanization in Africa: A Dissenting View." *African Geographical Review* 29 (2): 13–40.

Ochonu, Moses E. 2019a. "Looking for Race: Pigmented Pasts and Colonial Mentality in 'Non Racial' Africa." In *Relating Worlds of Racism: Dehumanisation, Belonging, and the Normativity of European Whiteness*, edited by Philomena Essed, Karen Farquharson, Kathryn Pillay, and Elisa Joy White, 3–37. London: Palgrave Macmillan.

———. 2019b. "Racism or Classism? Africa's Hidden Race Problem." *The Republic* 3 (1). https://republic.com.ng/vol3-no1/racism-or-classism.

Ofosu-Kusi, Yaw, and Esther Yeboah Danso-Wiredu. 2014. "Neoliberalism and Housing Provision in Accra, Ghana: The Illogic of an Over-Liberalised Housing Market." In *Selected Themes in African Development Studies: Economic Growth, Governance and the Environment*, edited by Lucky Asuelime, Joseph Yaro, and Suzanne Francis, 95–110. Advances in African Economic, Social and Political Development. Cham, Switzerland: Springer. https://doi.org/10.1007/978-3-319-06022-4_7.

Ogbamey, Alfred. 2002. "The Untold Story of 'Sodom and Gomorrah'." *The Nation*. October 11. https://www.ghanaweb.com/GhanaHomePage/NewsArchive/artikel.php?ID=28249.

Ohene, Elizabeth. 2020. "How Ghana Paid Tribute to George Floyd." *BBC News*, June 10, 2020. https://www.bbc.com/news/world-africa-52996849.

Okoye, Victoria. 2017. "Kantamanto Market: A Premier Destination for Secondhand Trade." *Smart Cities Dive*, March 18, 2017. https://www.smartcitiesdive.com/ex/sustainablecitiescollective/kantamanto-market-accra-premier-destination-secondhand-trade/129296.

Olaloku-Teriba, Annie. 2018. "Afro-Pessimism and the (Un)Logic of Anti-Blackness." *Historical Materialism* 26 (2). https://www.historicalmaterialism.org/article/afro-pessimism-and-the-unlogic-of-anti-blackness/.

Omotoso, Sharon Adetutu. 2018. "Gender and Hair Politics: An African Philosophical Analysis." *Journal of Pan African Studies* 12 (8): 5–19.

Opare, James Adu. 2003. "Kayayei: The Women Head Loaders of Southern Ghana." *Journal of Social Development in Africa* 18 (2): 33–48.

Otu, Kwame E., and Adriaan van Klinken. 2023. "African Studies Keywords: Queer." *African Studies Review* 66 (2): 509–30. https://doi.org/10.1017/asr.2022.163.

Owusu-Sekyere, Ebenezer, and Samuel Twumasi Amoah. 2020. "Urban Design, Space Economy and Survival in the City: Exploring Women's World of Work in Kumasi, Ghana." In *Sustainability in Urban Planning and Design*, edited by Amjad Almusaed, Asaad Almssad, and Linh Truong-Hong. https://www.intechopen.com/chapters/69440.

Oyěwùmí, Oyèrónké. 1997. *The Invention of Women: Making an African Sense of Western Gender Discourses*. Minneapolis: University of Minnesota Press.

———, ed. 2003. *African Women and Feminism: Reflecting on the Politics of Sisterhood*. Trenton, NJ: African World Press.

Page, Cara, and Erica Woodland. 2023. *Healing Justice Lineages: Dreaming at the Crossroads of Liberation, Collective Care, and Safety*. Berkeley, CA: North Atlantic Books.

Pierre, Jemima. 2012. *The Predicament of Blackness: Postcolonial Ghana and the Politics of Race*. Chicago: University of Chicago Press.

———. 2019. "The Racial Vernaculars of Development: A View from West Africa." *American Anthropologist* 122 (1): 86–98. https://doi.org/10.1111/aman.13352.

———. 2020. "Slavery, Anthropological Knowledge, and the Racialization of Africa." *Current Anthropology* 61 (S22): S220–S231. https://doi.org/10.1086/709844.

Plange, Nii-K. 1979. "Underdevelopment in Northern Ghana: Natural Causes or Colonial Capitalism?" In "The Roots of Famine," special issue, *Review of African Political Economy* 6 (15/16): 4–14.

Poole, Deborah. 1997. *Vision, Race, and Modernity: A Visual Economy of the Andean Image World.* Princeton, NJ: Princeton University Press.

———. 2005. "An Excess of Description: Ethnography, Race and Visual Technologies." *Annual Review of Anthropology* 34:159–79.

Prasse-Freeman, Elliott. 2020. "Resistance/Refusal: Politics of Manoeuvre Under Diffuse Regimes of Governmentality." *Anthropological Theory* 22 (1). https://doi.org/10.1177/1463499620940218.

Quashie, Kevin. 2012. *The Sovereignty of Quiet: Beyond Resistance in Black Culture.* New Brunswick, NJ: Rutgers University Press.

Quayson, Ato. 2020. *Oxford Street, Accra: City Life and the Itineraries of Transnationalism.* Durham, NC: Duke University Press.

Rattray, R. S. 1932. *The Tribes of the Ashanti Hinterland.* 2 vols. Oxford: Clarendon Press.

Reality Check Team. 2020. "African Diaspora: Did Ghana's Year of Return Attract Foreign Visitors?" *BBC News,* January 29, 2020. https://www.bbc.com/news/world-africa-51191409.

Reed, Ann. 2012. "The Commemoration of Slavery Heritage: Tourism and the Reification of Meaning." In *The Cultural Moment in Tourism,* edited by Laurajane Smith, Emma Waterton, and Steve Watson, 97–112. London: Routledge.

Reese, Ashanté. 2019. "Refusal as Care: Ethnography from Elsewhere." *Anthropology News,* June 4, 2019. https://doi.org/10.1111/AN.1181.

Riise, Mari Bakke. Director. *Kayayo- The Living Shopping Baskets.* Integral Film. 2016. 33 minutes. https://www.integralfilm.com/films/kayayo.

Roane, J. T. 2023. *Dark Agoras: Insurgent Black Social Life and the Politics of Place.* New York: New York University Press.

Robertson, Claire. 1983. "The Death of Makola Market and Other Tragedies." *Canadian Journal of African Studies* 17 (3): 469–95.

Robinson, Pat, et al. (1970) 2005. "A Historical and Critical Essay for Women in the Cities, June 1969." In *The Black Woman,* edited by Toni Cade Bambara, 251–67. New York: Washington Square Press.

Sekyiamah, Nana Darkoa. 2022. *The Sex Lives of African Women: Self-Discovery, Freedom, and Healing.* New York: Astra House.

Serpell, Namwali. 2020. "Unbothered: The Grace of Black Nonchalance." *Yale Review* 108 (4): 44–65.

Shah, Payal. 2015. "Spaces to Speak: Photovoice and the Reimagination of Girls' Education in India." *Comparative Education Review* 59 (1): 341–56.

Shange, Savannah. 2019. "Black Girl Ordinary: Flesh, Carcerality, and the Refusal of Ethnography." *Transforming Anthropology* 27 (1): 3–21.

Shankar, Arjun. 2016. "Auteurship and Image-Making: A (Gentle) Critique of the Photovoice Method." *Visual Anthropology Review* 32 (2): 157–66.

———. 2020. "Participation, Reception, Consent, and Refusal." In *The Routledge International Handbook of Ethnographic Film and Video,* edited by Phillip Vannini, 204–13. London: Routledge.

Sharpe, Christina. 2012. "Response to 'Ante-Anti-Blackness.'" *Lateral* 1. https://csalateral.org/issue/1/ante-anti-blackness-response-sharpe/.

———. 2014. "Black Studies: In the Wake." *Black Scholar* 44 (2): 59–69.

Shipley, Jesse Weaver, and Jemima Pierre. 2007. "The Intellectual and Pragmatic Legacy of Du Bois's Pan-Africanism in Contemporary Ghana." In *Re-Cognizing W. E. B. Du Bois in the Twenty-First Century: Essays on W. E. B. Du Bois*, edited by Mary Keller and Chester J. Fontenot Jr., 61–87. Macon, GA: Mercer University Press.

Shobat, Sara Cohen, and Christinia Landry, eds. 2018. *Rethinking Feminist Phenomenology: Theoretical and Applied Perspectives*. Lanham, MD: Rowman and Littlefield.

Shulist, Sarah, and Sameena Mulla. 2022. "Toward an Anthropology of Sexual Harassment and Power: Myth, Ritual, and Fieldwork." *American Anthropologist* (website), July 11, 2022. https://www.americananthropologist.org/online-content/toward-an-anthropology-of-sexual-harassment-and-power.

Simmons, Robert Ohene-Bonsu. 2018. "Disruptive Digital Technology Services: The Case of Uber Car Ridesharing in Ghana." Paper presented at the Twenty-Fourth Americas Conference on Information Systems, New Orleans, Louisiana.

Simone, AbdouMaliq. 2004. "People as Infrastructure: Intersecting Fragments in Johannesburg." *Public Culture* 16 (3): 407–29.

Simpson, Audra. 2007. "In Ethnographic Refusal: Indigeneity, 'Voice,' and Colonial Citizenship." *Journal for Thematic Dialogue* 9:67–80.

Smith, Christen A. 2015. "Blackness, Citizenship, and the Transnational Vertigo of Violence in the Americas." *American Anthropologist* 117 (2): 384–87.

———. 2016. *Afro-Paradise: Blackness, Violence, and Performance in Brazil*. Urbana: University of Illinois Press.

Smith, Christen A, Erica L. Williams, Imani A. Wadud, Whitney N.L. Pirtle and the Cite Black Women Collective. 2021. "Cite Black Women: A Critical Praxis (A Statement)." *Feminist Anthropology* 2 (1): 10–17.

Songsore, Jacob. 1989. "The Spatial Impress and Dynamics of Underdevelopment in Ghana." In *Inequality and Development: Case Studies from the Third World*, edited by Kenneth Swindell, J. M. Baba, and Michael J. Mortimore, 23–41. London: Commonwealth Foundation / Macmillan.

Spillers, Hortense. 1987. "Mama's Baby, Papa's Maybe: An American Grammar Book." *Diacritics* 17 (2): 65–81.

Spronk, Rachel, and S. N. Nyeck. 2021. "Frontiers and Pioneers in (the Study of) Queer Experiences in Africa: Introduction." *Africa* 91 (3): 388–97.

Star, Susan Leigh. 1999. "The Ethnography of Infrastructure." *American Behavioral Scientist* 43 (3): 377–91.

Stewart, Kathleen. 2007. *Ordinary Affects*. Durham, NC: Duke University Press.

———. 2017. "In the World That Affect Proposed." *Cultural Anthropology* 32 (2): 192–98. https://doi.org/10.14506/ca32.2.03.

Swanepoel, Natalie. 2009. "Every Periphery Is Its Own Center: Sociopolitical and Economic Interactions in Nineteenth-Century Northwestern Ghana." *International Journal of African Historical Studies* 42 (3): 411–32.

Táíwò, Olúfémi. 2010. *How Colonialism Preempted Modernity in Africa*. Bloomington: Indiana University Press.

Talton, Benjamin. 2010. *Politics of Social Change in Ghana*. London: Palgrave Macmillan.

Tamale, Sylvia, ed. 2011. *African Sexualities: A Reader*. Nairobi: Pambazuka Press.

———. 2020. *Decolonization and Afro-Feminism*. Ottawa: Daraja Press.

Tetteh, Benjamin. 2019. "2019: Year of Return for African Diaspora." *Africa Renewal*, December 2018–March 2019. https://www.un.org/africarenewal/magazine/december-2018-march-2019/2019-year-return-african-diaspora.

Thomas, Roger G. 1973. "Forced Labour in British West Africa: The Case of the Northern Territories of the Gold Coast 1906–1927." *Journal of African History* 14 (1): 79–103.

Thompson, Cheryl. 2009. "Black Women, Beauty, and Hair as a Matter of *Being*." *Women's Studies* 38 (8): 831–56.

Thorsen-Cavers, David William. 2006. "Entanglements: Tradition, Modernity & Globalization in Cape Coast." PhD diss., York University.

Tiernan, Han. 2021. "Archbishop Tutu Speaks Out Against Homophobia in Light of New Anti-LGBTQ+ Bill in Ghana." *GCN: Gay Community News*, November 29, 2021. https://gcn.ie/archbishop-tutu-against-homophobia-anti-lgbt-ghana/.

Trouillot, Michel-Rolph. 2003. *Global Transformations: Anthropology and the Modern World*. New York: Palgrave Macmillan.

Tsey, Komla. 2013. *From Head-Loading to the Iron Horse: Railway Building in Colonial Ghana and the Origins of Tropical Development*. Bamenda, Cameroon: Langaa Research and Publishing Common Initiative Group.

Tsikata, Dzodzi, and Wayo Seini. 2004. *Identities, Inequalities and Conflicts in Ghana*. CRISE Working Paper 5. Centre for Research on Inequality, Human Security and Ethnicity, University of Oxford, November.

Tynes, Brendane. 2020. "How Do We Listen to the Living?" *Anthropology News* (website), August 31, 2020. https://www.anthropology-news.org/articles/how-do-we-listen-to-the-living.

Wallace, Michelle. (1987) 1990. *Black Macho and the Myth of the Superwoman*. London: Verso.

Wang, Caroline, and Mary Ann Burris. 1997. "Photovoice: Concept, Methodology, and Use for Participatory Needs Assessment." *Health Education and Behavior* 24 (3): 369–87.

Whitehouse, Bruce. 2023. *Enduring Polygamy: Plural Marriage and Social Change in an African Metropolis*. New Brunswick, NJ: Rutgers University Press.

Wiemers, Alice. 2015. "A 'Time of Agric': Rethinking the 'Failure' of Agricultural Programs in 1970s Ghana." *World Development* 66 (February): 104–17.

———. 2017. "'It Is All He Can Do to Cope with the Roads in His Own District': Labor, Community, and Development in Northern Ghana, 1919–1936." *International Labor and Working-Class History* 92 (Fall): 89–113.

Williams, Bianca C. 2018. *The Pursuit of Happiness: Black Women, Diasporic Dreams, and the Politics of Emotional Transnationalism*. Durham, NC: Duke University Press.

Win, Everjoice J. 2009. "Not Very Poor, Powerless or Pregnant: The African Woman Forgotten by Development." *IDS Bulletin* 35 (4): 61–64.

Wingfield, Adia Harvey. 2008. *Doing Business with Beauty: Black Women, Hair Salons, and the Racial Enclave Economy*. Lanham, MD: Rowman and Littlefield.

Wooten, Terrance. 2021. "'The Streets Are My Home': Black Male Sex Offenders, Hypersurveillance, and the Liminality of Home." *Feminist Formations* 33 (1): 33–55.

Yeboah, Kwabena Agyare. 2019. "We Need to Talk About Ghana's Year of Return and Its Politics of Exclusion." *African Arguments*, December 19, 2019. https://africanarguments.org/2019/12/ghana-year-of-return-politics-of-exclusion.

INDEX

A1, 79
Abbas, 116–19, 121
Abossey Okai Central Mosque, 80
Accra Arts Centre, 50, 98–99
Accra General Post Office, 55, 69, 99
Accra Metropolitan Assembly (AMA), 9, 24, 52, 116, 143n8
activism, 14, 46, 48–49; feminist, 137n1; pleasure, 78; quiet, 140n20
Adamu, 34
affect, 3, 94, 106, 110–11, 122, 136n1; and modernity, 10–15, 131–32; and -ness, 39; and photovoice, 18, 64, 69, 73–75; racialized, 10–15, 40, 74, 143n6. *See also* emotions
affective economies, 18
Afful, Joseph Benjamin Archibald, 138n4
African Affairs Bureau, 46
African-American Association of Ghana, 48
African Americans, 46, 48, 83
Africana studies, 14
African brain drain, 8
African-descendant scholars, 12, 14, 74
African diaspora, 12, 32, 36, 64, 74, 130–32, 135n6, 137nn9–10; diasporic tourism, 41, 46–48, 53, 61; Ghana's role in, 38
African feminisms, 3, 12, 14–15, 20, 45, 48–49, 73–75, 91–92, 122, 128, 131–32
African Hebrew Israelites, 50
African studies, 12
Afrobeat, 115
Afrochella/AfroFuture, 46, 137n7
Afrophobia, 140n4. *See also* antiblackness
Agard-Jones, Vanessa, 142n16
Agbogbloshie, 1–2, 34, 80, 97, 105, 110, 121, 123
Agbogbloshie Market, 26, 116
agency, 20, 38, 45, 94, 112, 126, 128; household, 92; relationship, 92

Ahmed, Sara, 18
Airport City, 4
Airport Residential, 4
Aiyetoro Town, 32
Ajara, 34, 98–101, 103–6, 109–10
Akindele, Funke, 32
Akosua, Sister, 65–66
Akufo-Addo, Nana, 9, 45–48
Akuma Village, 50, 52–53, 97–98
Alien Compliance Order (1969), 8
Allah, 2
Alleyne, Osei, 137n10
Allied Agencies of Ghana, 25
Amadiume, Ife, 92
Amena, 1–2, 84–86, 98–99, 104–7, 109–10, 139n15, 143n6
Amera, 51–53, 61–62
androcentrism, 8, 26, 39, 43, 128
Angelou, Maya, 46
Ansah, Gladys Nyarko, 9
anthropology, 4, 28, 64, 74, 77, 96, 126, 128, 137n1; of Africa, 14, 73, 128, 132, 140n20; androcentric, 26; Black feminist, 18, 63; cultural, 35; of Ghana, 41–42; limits of, 69; North Atlantic hegemony in, 14; race in, 41–42. *See also* ethnography; fieldwork
anthropomorphism, 37
antiblackness, 14–15, 17, 39–41, 58, 61, 128, 130, 132, 136n1. *See also* Afrophobia
anti-hub of modernness, 12
Apapa Junction, 59
Armed Forces Revolutionary Council (AFRC), 27
Asante Market Women, 5
Asante people, 43, 45, 60
Asante Territory, 42
Asomaning, Vida, 7
aspirational ontology, 10

ACKNOWLEDGMENTS

This book is an index of pivotal points in adulting—the forging of lifelong friendships, torrid and terse relationships, galivanting through coffeehouses and nightlife on three continents, and the responses to calls of intuition and ancestors. I am indebted to so many people who have expanded and deepened my thinking throughout this project. There are likely to be people who have touched this project whose names I may have forgotten or missed. Please charge this oversight to my head and not my heart, which is exceedingly grateful.

To my kin folx and love people, there is no me without you. My mother, Tondalaya Harrison, told me that I was an anthropologist because I was *newsy* and loved to travel. Thank you for being my first Black feminist read, in all its permutations. My dad, Gary, gave me the "go-cut" of wonder and curiosity, and my brother James kept the fight for writing in me. Donald, your confidence shored me up when I lacked belief in myself. Dána, your encouragement helped me commit and complete. My children—baby Ruby, born with eyes open and ready for the world, and my chosen children, Kita and Francine, who embody the spirit of free Black children—are fiercely creative, loved, and beloved.

The formative experiences that forged this work began when I was an undergrad at Penn State and studied abroad at the University of Ghana, Legon. I remain thankful to my undergraduate adviser Christine Choi Ahmed, who insisted that an African and African American studies major needed to spend time on the continent. I am also appreciative of Professors Clement Abrokwaa, Nah Dove, and Clyde Woods for threading the disciplinary needle between Black studies and African studies in ways that continue to inform my thinking. I also thank Bernard Bell and Wilson J. Moses for their guidance to this first-gen student navigating the McNair Scholars Program.

A master's program at SOAS, University of London began my relationship with anthropology. With only an introductory cultural anthropology course in my intellectual toolkit, I cried through most of the first term of the anthropology lectures, but at least I learned how to argue about theory. I am ever grateful to Eva Omaghomi, the only other Black woman in the Anthropology of Media program, for schooling me on higher ed in the UK and introducing me to so many diasporic communities across the city. Living at Paul Robeson House in London, playing hearts in the kitchen with my flatmates Max and Khatija, attending Stuart Hall's Friday lectures at UCL, with Theoharis Papadakis and standing in lecture queues with Homa Khaleeli, Theoharis Papadakis, and Abigail Saffery were all nourishing experiences for this nerd.

By the time I started the PhD program in anthropology at Temple University, I felt shored up in epistemology and field experiences, but I had little understanding of cultural anthropology. Paul Stoller's commitment to storytelling as method kept me from dropping out. Black feminist ethnography and feminist anthropologists also mentored me through this project. In the sweltering heat of Florida in August, Dána-Ain Davis quelled my imposter syndrome and procrastination. Since her talk at a graduate seminar at Temple, Gina Ulysse reminded me to never lose focus on women as the center of ethnography. In a shared cab from an American Anthropological Association meeting to the airport, Lynn Bolles offered wisdom about ethnographic moments and self.

I have now visited Ghana for more than half of my life and, in many ways, Accra has raised me in a close second to Philadelphia. As such, I am in awe of and appreciate the generosity, grace, and friendship of so many people in Ghana. I hold close to the growing pains and life lessons I have learned and continue to learn there. I am grateful to the entire Azu family, especially the family matriarch, Aunty Alice Azu, for generously welcoming me and my family into their home for more than fifteen years. I have stepped out with a kind of courage that only comes from fierce friendships with spectacular women like Dedo, Maku and Mamle Azu, Maame Adjei, Naa Adzorkor Addo, and Ayeshatu Dugbartey. I have been intellectually fed by many Ghanaian women scholars, artists, and activists like Felicia Ansah Abban, Akosua Adomako Ampofo, Akosua Darkwah, and Nana Darkoa Sekyiamah.

This work could not exist without dedicated research assistants and collaborators, who have meticulously and earnestly transcribed and translated dialogue, helped me find my way in conversations, and smoothed my fumbles and faux pas: Idina Mumunia, Kwesi Bosomprah, Emmanuel Tommie, and Edna Owuor. I also thank my Twi tutors, Emmanuel Boateng and Perry Obeng, my favorite Kumasiano, Ernest Domfeh, as well as paddies Reggie Rockstone, Mensah Ansah, Nii Mantse Okyne, Black Prophet, Dufie Stony, and all the other folx who have shared dawn musings with me. Tetteh Kwarshie and Tiokor Nyakpemunya, thank you for walking all over Ghana with me, from Tamale to Aburi. Plus, you shadda me pass all!! I also appreciate Justice Hammond and his sister Stella for House No. 1, a refuge from Accra *wahala*, the scent of bougainvillea in every corner.

To the #diasporasdaughters, Du'Charm Archer, Natasha Boyce, and Dana Saxon, the squad of all squads; we make transhemispheric dance circles, hammocked daydreams, manifest milestones, and celebrate *The Plan*, over and over again. May we continue to stand under waterfalls and call on our ancestors, unknown and known, until we become old-old. Thank you to Beth Uzwiak; we have brewed, stewed, envisioned, and accomplied for decades; and my boughl Anthony Byron Carter, and #mvdf Memoria James.

I am thankful for so many writing groups in generative spaces, such as the Western Illinois University Write-In group with F. Erik Brooks, MaCherie Placide and Ron C. Williams, Davidson's Department of Africana Studies Friday writing group at Waterbean with Joseph Ewoodzie, Caroline Fache, Takiyah Harper-Shipman, Tracey Hucks, Hilton Kelly and Alice Wiemers; summer writing and socials with Natalie Deckard, Melissa Gonzalez, Rose Stremlau, and Patricia Tilburg; the sabbatigals, Amanda Martinez and Jane Mangan; cowriting with Akissi Britton, where we turned word pebbles into bricks; the chapter born through Nadine's bomb ass porridge, the #BFAM: Riché Daniel Barnes, Dawn Elissa Fischer, and Erica L. Williams; learning about fun productivity timers during brisk walks with Ashanté Reese; and chats with the other dope members of the inaugural Communications Collective of the Association of Black Anthropologists; Kaniqua Robinson, and Jamie A. Thomas.

Thank you to Jenny Tan and everyone at Penn Press; and to the anonymous reviewers for your labor—this is a better book as a result of your generous insights and constructive feedback.

This project has also benefited from support from the Woodrow Wilson Career Advancement Fellowship, Temple's dissertation completion grant, the

Minority Dissertation Fellowship at Western Illinois University, and numerous faculty study and research grants from Davidson College. I am also grateful for the year-long sabbatical afforded by the Boswell Family Fellowship at Davidson College and the resources provided by Dean Wendy Raymond and President Carol Quillen. Vanessa Victor, the departmental coordinator for the Anthropology department, has organizational skills and mother-friend energy that keeps me gathered. I am also gifted with friend-colleagues in Anthropology at Davidson—Brittany Brown, Helen Cho, John Cho, Fuji Lozada, Matt Samson, and Sam Shuman—as well as bright and inquisitive student scholars. I especially appreciate the students from the Davidson in Ghana study abroad programs, the summer 2023 cohort in particular, and specifically, Catherine Bennion, Maeve Corcoran, Walker Hansen, Idil Ira, AJ Jacobs, Kenzie Leonard, Anaya Patel, Sam Waithira, and Wiley White for reading chapter drafts and asking generative questions. I am exceedingly grateful to Nancy Fairley, the founder of the Ghana program, for her friendship, creativity and listening ear, whether sitting in the yard, or seaside in Cape Coast, Ghana.

Finally, there are no words that can hold the levels of gratitude, admiration, and wonder I have for the women and girls who have gifted me space in their lives since 2007. I am deeply indebted to the women from East Gonja, Tatale-Sanguli, Karaga, and Nanumba districts who have given me their time; to Sakina, Rahida, Fusena, Tani, Baiwa, Zahra, Karlikesu, Korkor, every Rama and Amina I know, Saylmana, Alheri, Azanzi, Balima, Dedei, Fuako, Yerda, Awa, Poko, Zaynab, Ajara, baby Shaibu (who is now a whole grown ass man), Nathaniel, Okaifor, Kwate, Amera, Ibrahim (the "shea butter shaman"), Kwei, Moses, Aunty Comfort, and every *kayayoo*, *kayanu*, and trader I have encountered at various markets in Ghana; from Makola, Agbogbloshie, Madina, Nima, Mankessim, Kejetia (KCM), Salaga, and night markets. To all the laborers in all these places, I am thankful for your candor, quick quips and catcalls (including *apuskeleke* and *obolo*), the dozens, as well as the shouting commentary of passersby that have ranged from caustic to kind. I have learned much from you all and I give thanks.

www.ingramcontent.com/pod-product-compliance
Lightning Source LLC
Chambersburg PA
CBHW030334270326
41926CB00010B/1615